MORE Household *Magic*

- Fast Cash In Your Attic
- Quick Clutter Cutters
- Live Rich (Even If You're Not)
- How To Pay Less For Everything

www.BottomLineSecrets.com

10 9 8 7 6 5 4 3 2 1

Printed in the United States of America

BHM/cg

CONTENTS

FAST CASH
IN YOUR ATTIC!

1

FAST CASH IN YOUR ATTIC!

RED-HOT COLLECTIBLES FOR LESS THAN $500

Source: **Malcolm Katt,** the owner of Millwood Gallery in Millwood, NY. An expert on collecting, he deals primarily in antique silver flatware and Nippon and Pickard porcelain. He has been a PowerSeller on eBay since 1998.

You don't have to spend a lot to build a spectacular collection. For $500 or less, you can buy some of today's hottest collectibles, ones that are reasonably priced and have appreciation potential.

VINTAGE TV SETS...

People collect TVs because they remind them of watching television back when it was a brand-new medium. Over the last five years, many early TVs (1940s to 1950s) have increased in value but are still affordable. Black-and-white, round-picture-tube sets with small screens (10" or less) are most likely to increase in value. Prices vary according to the scarcity of the set. Generally, it's desirable for collectible TVs to be working, but working and nonworking sets are equally valuable. You can find them at flea markets, yard sales and on-line (e.g., *www.harryposter.com* and *www.neweraantiques.com*). **EXAMPLES...**

- ***Crosley***—Model 9-420M (1949), 10" mahogany console, $75.
- ***General Electric***—Model 16K1 (late 1940s/early 1950s), 15" mahogany console with AM/FM radio and phonograph, $85.
- ***General Electric***—Model 21C2535 (1956), 20" mahogany telephone-dial tabletop/console with removable legs, $175.
- ***Motorola***—Model 7VT5 (1947), 7" portable with blond leatherette case, $245.
- ***Hallicrafters***—Model 505 (1947), 7" tabletop with push-button tuning and wood case, $395.

SUPER HOT: Philco Predictas, made between 1958 and 1960, have become some of the most desirable TVs. They feature a swivel picture tube and futuristic, atomic-age cabinet designs.

EXAMPLES: Model 3410 (Princess), 17" tabletop with metal grill and plastic tuner window, $400...Model 64242 (Holiday), 21" tabletop version, blond-finish wood cabinet, $475.

MORE INFORMATION: *Collector's Guide to Vintage Televisions: Identification & Values* by Bryan Durbal and Glenn Bubenheimer (Collector Books)...*www.harryposter.com/buy.htm*.

AD CHARACTERS...

As far back as the late 1800s, advertisers were using familiar characters to sell everything from tobacco to shoes. These characters, like Buster Brown, Mr. Peanut, Speedy Alka-Seltzer, Elsie the Cow and many others, appeared on billboards, in magazine ads and in grocery store aisles. Memorabilia depicting them has been sought by collectors for years and continues to be popular.

WHAT TO LOOK FOR: The main categories of vintage ad icons are packaging (e.g., cereal boxes), paper items (advertisements, postcards and store displays) and figurals (dolls, figurines, etc.).

PRICES: Pieces depicting ad characters, especially those dating back to the turn of the 20th century, have been appreciating for the past few years, yet nice examples for $500 and less are still available. **EXAMPLES...**

- ***1960s Mr. Peanut plastic charm bracelet, $30.****
- ***1950s Shoney's Big Boy 6" figural night-light with painted details, $115.***

*Prices reflect excellent, but not mint, condition.

• *1943 Borden ceramic salt and pepper shakers with Elsie the Cow, $150.*

• *1901 Buster Brown Shoes 2" celluloid pin depicting Buster and his dog, Tige, $310.*

• *1950s Speedy Alka-Seltzer clock with Speedy holding glass, $500.*

MORE INFORMATION: *Hake's Guide to Advertising Collectibles* by Ted Hake (Wallace-Homestead)...*www.advertisingiconmuseum.com/inside/collect.html.*

FISHER-PRICE TOYS...

Collectors hunt for vintage (1930s and 1940s) toys with the Fisher-Price red-and-white logo. You can buy decades-old pieces of all types—push toys, wind-ups and pull toys—for less than $100.

Old Fisher-Price toys look good because of the high-quality lithographed paper designs that are glued onto the wooden pieces. Prices have been rising for the past several years and the older toys, without the plastic parts added during the 1950s, should continue to appreciate.

1930s toys in good condition bring big prices ($1,000 to $3,000), but you can still find 1940s toys at reasonable prices. Condition is very important to value—ripped or soiled paper, missing parts or pieces, and broken mechanisms decrease a piece's worth. An original box always increases the value.

PRICES: The following are all animal figures with pull strings and lithographed paper designs glued onto wood...

• *1948 13½" Pony Chime with tin roller, $61.*

• *1946 13" Donald Duck xylophone, $220.*

• *1941 14¼" Dandy Dobbin (horse), $385.*

• *1942 12" Ducky Daddles (duck), $495.*

In 1959, Fisher-Price introduced one of the longest running toys of all time—the Play Family Little People. These were thumb-sized wooden figures that began appearing each year in different scenarios.

By the late 1960s, the Little People were being produced in plastic. Sets featuring the Little People are among the most sought after by collectors today, but prices are still reasonable. To be sure that you have a complete set, work with a knowledgeable dealer or the Fisher-Price Collectors Club, *http://groups.yahoo.com/group/FPCollectorsClub*. **EXAMPLES...**

- ***1970s Sesame Street Playhouse, $222.***
- ***1963 Amusement Park, $228.***
- ***1959 Safety School Bus, $295.***

MORE INFORMATION: *Fisher-Price: Historical, Rarity, and Value Guide, 1931–Present* by Bruce R. Fox and John J. Murray (Krause)...*www.thisoldtoy.com*.

DOMINO SETS...

Traditional dominoes were carved from bone or ivory with small pips (dots) of inset ebony. Many 19th-century sets were double-layered bone or ivory slabs pinned with brass to ebony slabs. Later, most dominoes were made of celluloid, Bakelite and other plastics and wood.

Collectors find dominoes appealing partly because vintage sets are readily available in myriad designs and materials. The standard domino set, called "double-six," has 28 pieces and contains every pairing of numbers between zero and six.

WHAT TO LOOK FOR: Complete sets with colorful graphics in their original, undamaged boxes.

EXAMPLES: Parker Brothers Washington Dominoes, issued in 1889, pictured George Washington and the Capitol...advertising dominoes that had their backs emblazoned with slogans—a circa 1940 set had the slogan, "Lord Calvert Whiskey For Those Of You Who Can Afford The Finest!"

PRICES: You can still find complete double-six boxed sets with appreciation potential at reasonable prices...

- ***Circa 1940 celluloid set in plastic case, $165.***
- ***Circa 1850 bone and ebony brass pinned set in original wood box, $235.***
- ***1920s Mail Pouch Dominoes,*** each domino marked on the back "Mail Pouch, High Grade Tobacco," with playing instructions, $500.

MORE INFORMATION: The Association of Game & Puzzle Collectors, *www.agpc.org*.

■

ON-LINE AUCTIONS: THE BEST STRATEGIES FOR BUYERS AND SELLERS

Source: **Dennis Prince,** CA-based author of several books about on-line auctions, including *AuctionWatch.com's Guide to Online Buying and Selling* and *Starting Your Online Auction Business* (both from Premier).

When should a seller use the "buy-it-now" option? What's the best way for a buyer to place a last-second bid? **HERE'S WHAT YOU NEED TO KNOW NOW...**

SELLERS...

• ***Stick with eBay except for certain items.*** There are other on-line auction sites (*www.bidz.com, www.auctions.amazon.com*), but they lag behind eBay's 212 million users. The more buyers there are, the more likely you'll get the fair market price or higher.

Several auction sites have significant volume in specific categories. Compare sales prices of items similar to yours at these sites and at eBay. **USE THE SITE THAT BRINGS THE HIGHER PRICES...**

• Computers and consumer electronics—*www.ubid.com* ...*www.dellauction.com* for Dell computers.

• Stamps—*http://stampauctionnetwork.com.*

• ***Use the buy-it-now option judiciously.*** For between five cents and 25 cents (depending on the cost of the item), eBay sellers can now offer buyers the option of preempting the auction by snapping up the item at a buy-it-now price named by the seller.

DOWNSIDE: If you set the price too high, you might discourage buyers from considering your item. If you set it too low, you might sell below market value.

Typically, the price is set at a slight premium to the amount similar items have fetched in the past.

Choose the buy-it-now option if...

• The category is hot, as Spider-Man comic books and collectibles were during the time of the movie's success.

• A gift-giving holiday is approaching.

• The item is the hardest-to-find component of a set. Buyers might be willing to pay a premium to complete their collections.

• ***Schedule the auction's close for a Sunday evening.*** Most eBay bids are placed in the final minutes of an auction, so you want to close when the greatest number of buyers are available. In my experience, that's Sunday evening at 9 pm Eastern time, 6 pm Pacific time. Saturday evening is the second-best option.

HELPFUL: Opt for a seven-day auction starting the previous Sunday evening. This gives people who log on only once a week a chance to see your item. Use a three- or five-day auction only if a gift-giving holiday is rapidly approaching—holiday buyers tend to want things right away.

BUYERS...

• ***Don't feel pressured to buy.*** So many people now sell on-line that even relatively rare items pop up with some frequency. There is never a need to overpay. If you lose one auction, another will come along.

• ***Know how to make a last-second bid.*** eBay auctions have what is known as a "hard close." When the auction period runs out, no more bids are accepted for that auction. Many smart buyers wait until the final seconds before making their moves, rather than bidding heavily earlier in the process and driving up the price.

A last-minute bid is always a gamble because you don't know how long you can wait to get your bid in. Sometimes, you can get a bid in when no time remains on the auction clock—other times, a bid with five seconds left on the clock is not accepted.

MY TRICK TO IMPROVE THE ODDS: I keep two windows open on my computer screen—one with my bid ready for submission, the other providing the status of the auction with the clock ticking down.

When the auction clock doesn't tick off each passing second—for example, when it jumps right from 25 seconds remaining directly to 23 or 22 seconds—it's an indication that eBay's servers are moving slowly. Then I know I had better get my bid in with five to seven seconds to spare if I want it to register before the auction is over.

If the servers are humming along, the clock will tick off each passing second, and I will put my bid in when there are three seconds left.

ANOTHER OPTION: Use a service from eSnipe.com, which makes your last-minute bid for you. You open a free (for the first 14 days) eSnipe account and type in the auction number and amount you wish to bid. If you win the auction, eSnipe charges a small fee to your credit card, usually 1% of the purchase price. You can use eSnipe only for bids on eBay.

Amazon.com has an auto-extension feature that makes last-second bids less effective. Auctions at this site end when no bids are made for a period of five minutes. In theory, an auction could go on forever.

• ***Search under misspellings.*** Savvy buyers have done this for years, but it bears repeating because the bargains can be big. Most shoppers search under the correctly spelled heading. There's less competition in an auction when the item description is misspelled.

EXAMPLES: I once found a *Poseidon Adventure* movie poster at a fraction of its usual cost by searching under "Posidon Adventure." The cheapest Beanie Babies are often sold as "Beenie Babies."

■

HOW TO SELL YOUR COLLECTIBLES FOR THE BEST PRICES

Sources: **Ralph** and **Terry Kovel,** Cleveland-based authors of 90 books on antiques, including *Kovel's Antiques and Collectibles Price List.* Random House Reference.

The prices you'll receive for collectibles depend on what, where and how you sell. The more you know about the value of what you're selling, the more successful you'll be.

VALUING THE UNKNOWN...

If you come into collectibles, say by inheritance, *never* throw anything out before finding out what it's worth. We've heard countless stories of people jettisoning stacks of magazines from the 1930s and 1940s or old costume jewelry in the belief that they couldn't be worth much. They find out later that the items were worth hundreds of dollars or more.

To learn the value of a collectible, ask a knowledgeable friend who collects what you have. Or use general on-line price guides—such as our *www.kovels.com*, which lists prices for more than 450,000 collectibles and antiques. Also look for specialized price guides at your local library for specific collectibles, such as Lladro, Hummel and Walt Disney ("Disneyana").

Collectors clubs and forums also allow you to see information about prices. The portal to these on-line sites is *www.collectorsresources.com*.

NOTE ON APPRAISALS: We don't generally recommend using a professional appraiser. They're costly—as much as $250 per hour—and a houseful of Grandma's things could take days to go through. Besides, 90% of the items are probably worth less than $100.

But, if you suspect that you have something valuable, it may be worth the cost. Contact the International Society of Appraisers (*www.isa-appraisers.org* or 888-472-4732) or the American Society of Appraisers (*www.appraisers.org* or 800-272-8258).

WHERE TO SELL...

- ***Garage or lawn sale.*** Withhold items with higher values that can fetch more at auction. Price the rest to sell quickly. This is the best way to go if you have little time and lots of cheap stuff to sell.
- ***Home sale.*** If you're disposing of the contents of a home, use the house itself to sell the furnishings.
- ***Antique stores.*** Dealers may buy your lot in total. But expect to receive no more than 50% of the listed value. Only if a piece is in mint condition and exceptional will they pay slightly more.
- ***Consignment shops.*** You collect what's received, minus the commission that is charged by the shop. Get a receipt for every item you consign with a description that includes any blemishes so you can keep track of what's sold and reclaim unsold items.
- ***Auction houses.*** Valuable items—$10,000 and up—often fetch the best prices through live auctions. Call a local auctioneer, or send photos and details, such as measurements, to major auction houses.

EXAMPLES: Sotheby's (*www.sothebys.com* or 800-813-5968) or Christie's (*www.christies.com* or 212-492-5485). Both have dozens of specialist departments running the gamut from ancient art to watches. International auction houses such as these will find the right venue for your collectible—for instance, a silver sale in London or a rare book sale in Amsterdam.

IMPORTANT: Get a copy of the auctioneer's business terms so that you'll know what commissions and fees you'll have to pay if your item is sold. Also, set a *reserve* (the minimum price you're willing to accept) on each piece.

• ***Internet auctions.*** There are two kinds of Internet auctions. In one, you sell items yourself at a site that just provides a place for you to list them. The heavyweights for this kind of auction are eBay (*www.ebay.com*) and Amazon.com Auctions (*www.auctions.amazon.com*). While a live auction may attract several hundred potential buyers, on-line sites draw thousands. All sites make you register and pay both a listing fee and a selling fee on successful auctions.

NOTE: Only about 30% or less of the items that are listed actually sell.

ALTERNATIVE: Internet auction sites that function the same way as large auction houses at an actual physical location—they even have catalogs available ahead of the auction date. Bidding may take place just on the Internet, or on the Internet at the same time as people bid at a physical location. These auction sites are good for certain collectibles, such as sports memorabilia, stamps, coins and toys. Go to *www.vendio.com* to find sites that specialize in your collectibles category. There are additional specialized sites, including *www.mastronet.com* for sports memorabilia and *www.bertoiaauctions.com* for toys and dolls.

• ***Collectibles magazines.*** You can place an ad in specialized magazines and antique newspapers. This is a low-cost way to sell your collectibles and, hopefully, get top dollar—you're marketing directly to interested buyers. Make your ad short and to the point. Be sure that it honestly represents the item.

EXAMPLES: Antique Trader (*www.antiquetrader.com* or 800-258-0929) has national coverage and lists shows...Maine Antique Digest (*www.maineantiquedigest.com* or 877-237-6623) gives a lot of interesting gossipy detail...and Antique Week (*www.antiqueweek.com* or 800-876-5133) reports on what has happened and what's ahead.

IMPORTANT: Receive payment before you ship. Shipping is your responsibility. Insure your item when you ship it. United Parcel Service (UPS) offers some insurance, but you may need to get more.

NOTE: When insuring through the postal service, we have found that it's difficult to collect from them if something happens to the package.

• ***Internet classifieds.*** Like collectibles magazines and newspapers, this venue lets you list for free or a small charge. TIAS.com (*www.tias.com*), an on-line antique mall with more than 1,000 dealers, has 200,000 readers of its on-line collectibles newsletter.

• ***Swap shows.*** Rent a table at your local collectibles "trade and swap" show—you'll find listings in your local newspaper, on the Internet or through your chamber of commerce. This venue requires some time and preparation, but you can make lasting contacts with dealers and collectors. Price everything before you set up.

IMPORTANT: Know the lowest you'll go on each item.

SHARE WITH UNCLE SAM...

Don't ignore income tax on collectibles. As long as you've held an item for more than one year (or inherited it), gain is taxed at up to 28%. Collectibles gains don't qualify for the 15% capital gains rate.

STRATEGY: If you inherit something you plan to sell, do so sooner rather than later. (Your basis for figuring gain is its value at the time of the person's death.) If the value declines, you'll have a loss that you can't deduct. There's no loss allowed for tax purposes on the sale of personal items.

■

FIND OUT WHAT YOUR COLLECTIBLES ARE WORTH ON-LINE

Source: **Malcolm Katt,** the owner of Millwood Gallery in Millwood, NY. An expert on collecting, he deals primarily in antique silver flatware and Nippon and Pickard porcelain. He has been a PowerSeller on eBay since 1998.

Thanks to the success of the on-line auction site eBay, which holds hundreds of collectibles auctions every hour, collectors who previously relied on guidebooks to determine collectible values now use real-time on-line prices for greater accuracy.

eBay auctions have redefined "scarcity"—many collectibles once thought to be rare are quite common, and prices are reduced due to the increased supply. Rely on "field-based" values (prices that buyers are actually paying). To check the recent price history of a collectible, go to *www.ebay.com* and click on "Advanced Search," then mark the box next to "Completed Listings Only." If you insure your collectibles, stay current with eBay prices and periodically adjust coverage based on the market value of your collection.

■

QUICK CLUTTER CUTTERS!

2

QUICK CLUTTER CUTTERS!

FENG SHUI LESSONS TO MINIMIZE STRESS IN YOUR HOME

Source: **Angel Thompson,** a Marina del Rey, CA, design consultant who uses feng shui in her work with clients. She is the author of *Feng Shui: How to Achieve the Most Harmonious Arrangement of Your Home and Office*. St. Martin's Griffin.

What in the world is *feng shui*? It's an ancient Chinese system for creating harmony within your home.

Although the philosophy underlying feng shui is extremely complex—and hard for many Americans to grasp—my experience with it suggests that it really does work.

Set up your household according to a few basic principles, and you should find your life far less stressful. As we know from countless mind–body studies, anything that reduces stress is good for your health.

Here's what to do…

• ***Make sure your home's entrance is inviting.*** Coming home to a broken gate or a front door with peeling paint has a depressing effect.

Don't put up with such problems. Fix what needs fixing. Install welcoming lights. Add a fresh coat of paint or a colorful doormat. Hang a decorative bell or nameplate.

• ***Get rid of clutter.*** Is your home filled with stacks of old newspapers and piles of clothes you've been meaning to give away? Do your bookshelves groan under the weight of books you'll never read?

Clutter drags down your spirits and creates a subtle but pervasive sense that your household is out of control.

Get rid of everything you don't want or need. That includes items given to you by friends or family.

If you cannot bring yourself to throw out a gift you received from an old friend, store it in a closet until the friend comes for a visit.

• ***Make sure your home is well lighted.*** Keep windows, blinds and drapes scrupulously clean. Burned-out bulbs should be replaced right away—even if there are other light sources in the room.

• ***Arrange seating carefully.*** In many homes, seats are arranged so that people sitting on them face a wall. This creates a "boxed-in" feeling.

Go from room to room and try out every seat in your home. Make sure each is placed in such a way that someone sitting on it is facing as much open space as possible.

• ***Confine old family photos to a single area.*** Scattering old photos all over the house forces you to reminisce all day long.

Whether the memories triggered by the photos are pleasant or not, you're better off if you don't dwell on them too often.

Find a hallway or another out-of-the-way spot to hang old pictures. Recent photos can go in the rooms where you spend the most time.

• ***Fill your home with greenery.*** Plants provide a sense of energy and vitality.

Position them so that they're at many different heights—just as they would be in a forest. This gives a natural, soothing feel to any room.

• ***Consider getting an aquarium or a miniature waterfall.*** Water in motion—whether it's rippling over rocks or eddying around fish as they swim—has a uniquely calming effect.

One easy aquarium setup would be to have two goldfish and one black fish.

Tabletop waterfalls range from simple models costing about $25 to elaborate models selling for more than $500.

• ***Enliven your home with mirrors.*** Mirrors give the illusion of greater spaciousness. They catch and reflect light, too.

Be sure the tallest person in the family can see his/her head in each mirror. It's disquieting to see a "decapitated" image of yourself as you walk by.

Do *not* hang a mirror directly opposite an entrance. A guest entering your home should be able to peer directly into the foyer or the first room—not see his own reflection.

■

CLUTTER CONTROL

Source: **Leslie Walden,** professional organizer and founder of It's Time To Get Organized, an Atlanta-based organizing firm. *www.itstimetogetorganized.com.*

Even the best-designed closet can get messy if you don't control your "stuff." **HERE'S HOW...**

• ***Sort through your wardrobe and give away things that you rarely wear.*** Fewer clothes means less time wasted each morning searching for what to wear. Crowded closets look messy no matter how nice your fixtures...and hanging clothes tend to wrinkle when they're packed in tightly.

If discarding unloved clothes does not create much space, move out-of-season items to a guest room closet or attic. If your attic gets hot, avoid storing clothes in plastic bags from dry cleaners—the heat may melt the bags.

BEST: Wrap clothes in pillowcases or sheets and store in a cedar trunk.

In the future, each time you buy a new article of clothing, remove one old item from your closet.

• ***Select the closet components that best match your needs.*** Cubbies can organize shoes...a chain with clips holds hats...wall hooks keep purses out of the way.

Double-hung rods maximize closet space by adding a second row of hangers below the first. Only dresses, coats and robes need the full vertical space offered by single rods.

• ***Group clothes by type***—put all polo shirts together, all suits together—or by outfit, if you tend to wear the same pieces together repeatedly.

• ***Designate a space for clothes that need to be washed or dry-cleaned.*** Arrange your closet components so that the clothes you wear most are easiest to reach.

• ***Box and label items on closet shelves.*** Keep a folding ladder in your closet for easy access. The Container Store's Slim Folding Step Stool collapses to just 1.5 inches in width for easy storage (888-266-8246, *www.containerstore.com*, $39.99). ■

ORGANIZING FROM THE INSIDE OUT

Source: **Julie Morgenstern,** founder of Julie Morgenstern Enterprises, whose clients include the New York City mayor's office, Time Warner and the Miami Heat basketball team, *www.juliemorgenstern.com*. She is author of *Organizing from the Inside Out*. Owl Books.

What keeps you from getting organized? It's not sloppiness, laziness or incompetence. **ODDS ARE YOU'RE HELD BACK BY ONE OR MORE PSYCHOLOGICAL OBSTACLES, SUCH AS...**

• ***Need for abundance.*** You may have a deep-rooted need for possessions. Your need for abundance could have evolved from deprivation as a child. The thought of getting rid of anything fills you with anxiety.

Do not try to overpower this need by throwing things out. You will just start collecting again. Instead, learn to organize your stuff.

• ***Need to conquer chaos.*** You might like your spaces disorganized because you love to create order out of chaos. You might have developed this as a survival skill from having grown up in challenging circumstances.

Try redirecting your talent for fixing things. Use your free time to focus on more meaningful tasks.

• ***Sentimental attachment.*** When items have special meaning, it's hard to let them go. These things may represent another time, person or part of yourself that you feel will be lost forever if you let go. When objects define you, you wind up living amidst clutter.

Your identity comes from inside, not outside. Although objects serve as reminders, your memories of the past are inside you, too. Get rid of objects that are no longer an *active* part of your life, such as old clothing, and papers and other items from college, a former career, a dead spouse, etc.

STRATEGY: If it's difficult for you to throw things out, move some of the old stuff to an attic, basement, garage or rental storage facility.

PURGING...

My system of organizing focuses not on getting rid of things but on identifying what is important to you and finding homes for these items. Define what items are essential to your home or job so you'll have direction in sorting and purging. **HOW...**

• ***Identify "big picture" goals.*** Decide what really matters to you—joy, satisfaction, accomplishment. Then test each item against your goal by asking yourself, "Will this help me to further my goal?" Keep only "yes" items.

• ***Use the 80/20 rule.*** You use only 20% of what you own—the balance are things you once used, feel you should use or think you might someday use.

If you have trouble identifying the 20%, once a month stick a red adhesive dot on every object you handle every time you handle it. Also put a dot on every knickknack that makes you feel good when you look at it. After a month, you'll know which items really count, making purging a breeze.

• ***Sort, purge, assign a home to, put in containers and maintain your system.*** Do every step in order—sort, then purge and so on.

In purging, you can choose to toss out, give away, sell, put elsewhere or store. "No-brainers"—items in bad shape and worthless to others—should be thrown away.

To motivate yourself to purge, think about what you will gain—more space for things you use and love...more time (by not having to search through clutter)...more money (you can sell items of value or donate them to charity for a possible tax deduction)...and more satisfaction (by giving items to family, friends or charity).

CAUTION: Check with your accountant, lawyer or office manager for retention guidelines on tax and legal papers.

If you use a file system at work, put a pencil dot in the upper right corner of each file folder every time it's used. Once a year, review your "dots." Throw out or archive folders with no dots.

NO-BRAINER TOSS LISTS...

At the office...

- ***Product solicitations***—if you're not ready to buy right now.
- ***Old magazines, books and articles***—if you haven't looked at them in at least 12 months.
- ***Old research materials***—keep the source, not the paper. Maintain a list of sources in your Rolodex.
- ***Duplicates of documents***—keep the original in a plastic sleeve and no more than one copy.
- ***Early drafts of proposals***—retain only the final version.
- ***Supplies***—get rid of supplies you don't use.

In a home office...

- ***Information you already know***—save only new information you can learn from.
- ***Outdated vendor brochures***—again, keep the source in your Rolodex, not the paper.
- ***Stationery you no longer use***—keep one sheet in a job-history file and toss the rest.
- ***Old receipts, bank statements, auto records***—toss unless needed for tax purposes.

At home...

- ***Junk mail and old catalogs.***
- ***Expired warranties.***
- ***Grocery receipts, invitations to past events and recipes*** you haven't tried in five years, if ever.
- ***Business cards from people*** you don't remember.
- ***Clothing/linens that are stained,*** torn or no longer fit.
- ***Broken tools,*** appliances, furniture, dishes.
- ***Mildewed or moth-eaten items*** and dried-out paint.
- ***Obsolete baby equipment.***
- ***Old college textbooks.***
- ***Expired medicines.***
- ***Games, books, compact discs and cassettes you haven't played,*** read or listened to in years or that are damaged.

SUGGESTION: It can be hard to toss items of children who have grown up. So save the best of these by creating a memory box—a time capsule of a *limited* number of keepsakes (drawings, report cards, awards, etc.). Take pictures of items too large to fit (old team jersey, a shelf of trophies).

DOWNSIZING...

Moving to a smaller space can be challenging. **YOU NEED TO...**

• ***Analyze.*** Take stock of your current situation (where you are, where you're going, what's holding you back) and why it's important to downsize.

• ***Strategize.*** Create a plan for transforming your space.

• ***Attack.*** Sort, purge, assign a home to, put in containers, maintain your system.

• ***Store.*** Downsizing may mean storing some things temporarily—until you gain a clear picture of your new space or because you can't part with some items. **SOME WAYS TO ACCOMMODATE YOUR THINGS...**

• Add storage units—some furniture (end tables, for example) can act as storage units.

• Make better use of shelf space—move shelves closer to each other, stack things.

• Install floor-to-ceiling shelves.

• Store items in bins under beds and below garments hanging in closets.

■

STRATEGIES FOR CONTROLLING CLUTTER

Source: **Lorraine Chalicki,** organizing consultant, clutter-clearing specialist and owner, YouNeedMe.com, Seattle.

If you collect keepsakes, keep just *one* that best represents a particular time or occasion.

• ***Set a specific goal to encourage*** you to arrange things. **EXAMPLE:** An organized kitchen makes preparing meals easier.

• ***Start with a single room.*** Finish that area before moving on.

• ***Create specific places for things*** so they do not wind up all over the place.

EXAMPLE: A place where the mail always goes until you have time to sort it.

■

DROWNING IN STUFF? SMART WAYS TO GET RID OF IT

Source: **Julie Morgenstern,** founder of Julie Morgenstern Enterprises, whose clients include the New York City mayor's office, Time Warner and the Miami Heat basketball team, *www.juliemorgenstern.com*. She is author of *Organizing from the Inside Out*. Owl Books.

The next time you're about to put off the task of tossing out old possessions, consider the advantages of...

• ***More room to enjoy your home.*** An uncluttered house or apartment is easier to keep clean, easier to entertain in and just more pleasant to be in.

• ***Better organization.*** Hunting for objects takes time and causes anxiety, especially when the object is important, such as a document or treasured gift. Organizing and finding items are easier when you have fewer of them.

• ***Bringing joy to friends and relatives and even strangers in need.*** More people than you realize may want the possessions you no longer need.

• ***Lower taxes.*** By giving unwanted objects to a charity, you may be eligible for an income tax deduction.

• ***Profits.*** When you sort through your possessions, you occasionally find items that are surprisingly valuable.

OVERCOMING HURDLES...

Despite the benefits of throwing out unneeded possessions, many of us shrink from the task.

The biggest obstacle is the guilt that many people feel when they discard objects that came from a beloved relative. Guilt can also be strong in individuals who inherited a Depression-era mentality of saving every item that might possibly be of use in the future.

Guilt can nearly always be overcome by giving unneeded items to other family members who will treasure them or to people who can genuinely use them. An old picture frame, for example, may be useless to you but treasured by a relative who knew that it came from a great-grandparent.

Don't think just of relatives but also of friends and children of friends. A neighbor's child, for instance, may be in college, where he/she might be able to use the old couch that's been taking up space in your basement.

Fear is the other big hurdle that often prevents people from throwing out unneeded possessions. Fear typically affects those who feel more secure when they're surrounded by a trove of familiar objects.

Overcome fear by concentrating on what the effort will allow you to do—all the benefits mentioned above.

Many families hesitate to throw away objects for fear that they might be valuable. If that's the case in your home, settle the issue by getting them appraised. Once you know the actual value, you can make an informed decision about keeping the item or selling it.

Professional appraisers usually charge $100 to $350 per hour and can evaluate about 10 items in an hour. To find an appraiser, ask your bank, attorney or insurance agent.

GETTING THE JOB DONE...

STEP 1: Go through your house room by room, and examine each possession. Ask yourself, *Do I use this object? Do I love it?* If you don't answer *yes* to either question, it's time to discard the item.

STEP 2: Put a tag on each item you want to discard. Use tags of different colors to indicate the specific way you intend to dispose of the object.

EXAMPLE: A red tag for items to be thrown away, green for charities, blue for gifts, etc.

STEP 3: Begin disposing of items. Cart them to the trash, contact people you want to give them to or ask charities to take the items away.

If the job looks too daunting—or if you get bogged down once you start—ask for help from a friend or relative, or hire someone to assist. Many high school students, for example, would be eager for the $5 an hour you might offer.

CAUTION: Before disposing of any object, examine it thoroughly. You may occasionally find money, jewelry or other valuables that have long been forgotten in pockets of clothing, drawers of furniture and even pages of books.

For charitable donations, IRS rules are tricky, so give to a well-known organization or consult with your accountant or tax preparer to find out if the charity is qualified and the rules about receipts and other documentation.

OFF-SITE STORAGE...

For most people, renting a long-term storage unit is rarely worth the $60 a month that even a small space is likely to cost. But there are exceptions.

EXAMPLE: Individuals with small apartments who inherit a houseful of items for which they have no room.

People in doubt about throwing away a large number of possessions are another exception. For them, it can make sense to put the objects in a storage facility for a limited time, such as three months.

If they don't need any of the items during that time, it will then be much easier to get rid of them.

KEEP CLUTTER AWAY...

To keep yourself from accumulating unwanted possessions in the future...

• ***As mentioned earlier, periodically look at items in your house*** and then ask yourself the two basic questions—*Do I use this object? Do I love it?* Unless you answer *yes* to either one, dispose of the object immediately.

• ***Each time you make a purchase, look for an item to throw away.*** All too often, when we buy a new jacket, blouse or pair of shoes, we miss the opportunity to dispose of an old one we haven't worn for years.

There's an even greater opportunity to discard household furnishings, such as table lamps, whenever we buy a new one.

■

WHERE TO SEND YOUR STUFF

Source: **Julie Morgenstern,** founder of Julie Morgenstern Enterprises, whose clients include the New York City mayor's office, Time Warner and the Miami Heat basketball team, *www.juliemorgenstern.com.* She is author of *Organizing from the Inside Out.* Owl Books.

Lighten the task of getting rid of clutter by contacting the following organizations...

• ***A charity that picks up donated goods,*** such as Goodwill Industries (800-664-6577, *www.goodwill.org*) or the Salvation Army (*www.salvationarmyusa.org*, check your local directory for a telephone number).

• ***An organization that finds nonprofit organizations in your area*** that want the specific goods you want to donate. In most cases, the nonprofit will then collect the items.

ONE OF THE BEST KNOWN: Excess Access (415-242-6041, *www.excessaccess.com*).

• ***A removal service such as 1-800-GOT-JUNK?*** (800-468-5865, *www.1800gotjunk.com*). The company's rates are generally low, although they vary from area to area.

■

LIVE RICH! (EVEN IF YOU'RE NOT)

3

LIVE RICH! (EVEN IF YOU'RE NOT)

THERE ARE WAYS TO GET GOOD SEATS TO SOLD-OUT EVENTS

Sources: **Dale Ratermann,** former executive director of the Pacers Foundation, a nonprofit charitable group founded by the NBA's Indiana Pacers, and **Mark Andrew Zwartynski,** The Mark Andrew Group, a sports marketing firm. They are coauthors of *Two on the Aisle: How to Get Tickets to Any Event, Anytime, Anywhere.* Masters Press.

The best seats to most events—whether it is a Broadway show, a popular concert or a professional sports event—often go to corporate clients or friends of the performers.

But there are ways that anyone can get great seats—even when the box office tells you the event is sold out.

• ***Invest in a package deal.*** Choice seats in most stadiums, arenas and concert halls often go to subscribers or season ticket holders.

Buying a package also guarantees the holder an opportunity to buy tickets for special events, such as postseason play-off games.

Most people aren't aware that they don't have to commit to the *maximum* number of home games or all of the concert season's Friday nights. A partial package will likely get you most of the same benefits.

One way to cut the cost of a limited ticket package is to share the cost with friends.

HELPFUL: Your own lottery for special events with names drawn out of a hat to avoid disagreements.

• ***Buy tickets at the last minute.*** When a computerized seller, such as Ticketmaster, tells you over the phone that a show or game is sold out, do not despair. Even the hottest events release tickets on the day of the performance, often with the best seat locations. These tickets may have been held for performers who couldn't use them...season ticket returns...or bad credit card orders.

These late-released tickets for sporting events and large-scale concerts usually go back into the inventories of computerized ticket sellers. For theater and opera, you may need to go directly to the box office.

HELPFUL: Check three hours before the performance to see if any tickets have been released. Then check again one hour before...and again at show time. It is not unheard of for tickets to be released a few minutes after a performance has begun.

BROADWAY STRATEGY: Pick three sold-out Broadway shows that you would like to see. Then make the rounds of all three box offices on the day of the performances...and do it again and again in the hours leading up to showtime.

• ***Be willing to sit by yourself.*** Long after pairs of tickets are sold out, single seats are often still available.

IMPORTANT: When the only seats that are next to each other are in terrible locations, you usually can do much better by buying separate seats.

Catch up with your partner during intermissions and after the final curtain. After all, you don't communicate much during performances anyway.

• ***Beat the crowds.*** When tickets to a hot event go on sale through a computerized ticket vendor, the phone lines become swamped. To avoid an endless busy signal, start calling an hour earlier than the listed time. If the operators are ready to work, they may take your order.

HELPFUL: Try the local number for the vendor in case the 800 number is busy. It also takes less time to redial seven numbers locally than the 11 needed in the 800 number.

• ***Try ticket vendors' off-site locations,*** which are usually located inside record, department and souvenir stores. While you may have to pay a small charge, the crowds are likely to be smaller than at the box office.

Unlike the box office, off-site outlets generally accept only cash, not credit cards. That means faster lines.

• ***Attack on two fronts.*** While waiting in line at a ticket outlet, use your cell phone to reach the outlet's operators. If you get through before reaching the head of the line, you will have reserved better seats than everyone else standing in front of you.

• ***Order tickets through the Internet.*** While using your computer won't allow you to reach a computerized vendor faster than by calling, you will be better prepared to buy the seats you want.

The types of information available at vendor Web sites include starting times...price ranges...and maps that show seat locations—information that a telephone seller may be too busy to provide.

When buying from a ticket broker, hold out for the best possible deal. For especially tough tickets, like the Super Bowl or the NBA Finals, ticket brokers in the city of the event may demand five or 10 times the face value of the tickets.

GOOD NEWS: Their asking prices often are negotiable or may even drop due to sluggish last-minute demand.

HELPFUL: Call three brokers to compare prices. If all of the prices quoted seem too high, be patient—check back...and back again. If the demand for tickets falls short of expectations, asking prices may nosedive shortly before the event.

■

HOW TO GET THE BEST TABLES IN RESTAURANTS

You can get better restaurant tables by making reservations through a hotel concierge.

REASON: The restaurant wants the hotel to continue to recommend it to customers, so it keeps the hotel guests happy by giving them the best seats.

■

HOW TO MAKE PEOPLE LIKE YOU IN 90 SECONDS OR LESS

Source: **Nicholas Boothman,** licensed practitioner of neurolinguistic programming, a branch of applied psychology devoted to the improvement of communications skills. He first developed an interest in the field when he was a photographer and needed to establish instant rapport with his subjects. Based in Ontario, Canada, he is author of *How to Make People Like You in 90 Seconds or Less.* Workman. His Web site is *www.nicholasboothman.com.*

People decide if they like you within two seconds of meeting you. **HERE IS HOW TO MAKE SURE YOUR FIRST IMPRESSION IS A GOOD ONE...**

• ***Smile.*** If you are worried that your smile doesn't look natural, try standing six inches from a mirror and saying the word "great" in funny voices. This will almost certainly make you smile. The next time you meet someone, think *great.* A natural smile will form.

• ***Notice eye color.*** This ensures that you are meeting the other person's gaze. Poor eye contact suggests that you have something to hide. But don't stare—it may make him/her uncomfortable. Oddly enough, occasionally looking at your hands conveys the impression of active listening.

• ***Use "open" body language.*** Keep your arms uncrossed and hands unclenched. If you are unsure of what to do with your hands, put them in your back pockets or at your sides.

Point your heart toward the heart of the other person.

• ***Mirror the other person's gestures and body language.*** People take an instant liking to those who are similar to themselves. If you meet someone who is loud and talks with his hands, be equally loud and use the same gestures. If the person laughs a lot, do the same.

This technique can even defuse a hostile situation. A corporate student of mine was one of three people berated by an important client, the intimidating owner of a large grocery store chain. The bully's other two targets meekly apologized. That only made the client angrier.

My student "matched" the client. Using similar arm gestures and a similarly raised voice, he told the man that he was absolutely right—that they had let him down. Within minutes, the client had his arm around my student's shoulder.

HELPFUL: After a few moments of matching, change your movements. If the other person follows suit, he feels in sync with you. If not, continue matching movements and try again. If you are dealing with an angry person, gradually lower your voice and open your body language. If you are speaking with someone who seems bored, lean forward and see if he becomes more animated.

• ***Ask open-ended questions.*** Who, what, where, when, why and how questions are conversation starters. Questions that begin with *Have you...?*, *Are you...?* and *Do you...?* are conversation killers. They can be answered with one word—*yes* or *no*.

• ***Relax.*** A Princeton University study found that trying too hard to be liked is a big turnoff in first encounters. Before you have to meet someone, take a few deep abdominal breaths to relax. When you are nervous, you take shallow breaths. This makes your voice high-pitched and shaky. Deep breaths make your voice richer and more confident.

■

DECORATING FOR NEXT TO NOTHING

You want your home to look better than it does, but spending thousands of dollars to hire a decorator and buying new furniture is out of the question. What do you do?

Professional room arrangers create a new look using the furniture and accessories you already possess. They typically charge $100 per hour...$300 to $500 per room.

We asked six interior arrangers to share their favorite decorating tricks...

ARRANGING FURNITURE...

• ***Find the room's natural focal point.*** Most rooms have an architectural feature that draws the eye—often a window or fireplace. Arrange furniture around that feature. If you add an additional focal point, such as a TV, position it near the architectural focal point.

• ***Separate "heavy" furniture.*** If a room contains a dark armoire and a dark-colored couch, place them on opposite sides of the room. Left together, they can make a space feel unbalanced.

From: **Joanne Hans,** owner, A Perfect Placement, an interior-arrangement firm in Mechanicville, NY, *www.aperfectplacement.com.*

• ***Turn an oversized room into two or more activity areas.*** If a room is so large that you can't have a comfortable conversation sitting at opposite ends, turn a corner into its own cozy space with two chairs and a table arranged for private conversation.

From: **Sarah Susanka,** Raleigh, NC–based author of *Not So Big Solutions for Your Home.* Taunton. Her Web site is *www.notsobighouse.com.*

• ***Pull the sofa away from the wall.*** Then put a table behind it to create depth and interest. The table should be just a bit shorter than the couch and 12 inches deep. Because the table will be hidden behind the sofa—and perhaps covered with a cloth—even a cheap table will do. Sears and JC Penney have them for about $100. Top them with plants, books and framed photos. If the table is not hidden, put a basket with a fern underneath.

From: **Gina March,** owner of the St. Louis–based interior rearrangement firm It's Your Stuff Room Redesigns.

• ***Borrow from the dining room if you don't have enough seating in the living room.*** Many dining-room sets come with two armchairs that sit unused. It's perfectly acceptable to put these chairs elsewhere in the house. Borrow from other rooms, too. A nightstand can become an end or hall table. A bathroom mirror can be used in the hall.

From: **Wendy Dilda,** president, Realty Enhancements International, Rancho Santa Margarita, CA, *www.realtyenhancement.com.*

• ***Never position furniture so you have to walk around it to enter a room.*** It makes the room uninviting.

WINDOWS...

• ***Buy curtain rods that are up to three feet wider than the windows.*** Hang curtains that cover the extra inches on each side. This makes a room look grander. Hang the curtain rod higher than the top of the window—this makes the ceiling appear higher, too.

From: **Chayse Dacoda,** a featured designer on TLC's room-makeover series *While You Were Out.* She runs Dacoda Design in Los Angeles and New York City, *www.dacodadesign.com.*

RUGS...

• ***Put an angled area rug in a small room.*** Small rooms can be a decorating challenge because they often leave few options—you might have no choice but to push all of the furniture up against the walls. To add interest, place an area rug at an angle to the dimensions of the room. Area rugs can be placed on wall-to-wall carpeting as well as on wood or tile floors.

From: **Judy Alto,** owner, Interior Expressions, in Annapolis, MD.

■

SCENTS TO BOOST ENERGY, MOOD, MEMORY AND MORE

Source: **Alan Hirsch, MD,** assistant professor, department of neurology and psychiatry, Rush-Presbyterian-St. Luke's Medical Center, and founder and neurological director, The Smell & Taste Treatment and Research Foundation, *www.scienceofsmell.com,* both in Chicago. He is author of *Life's a Smelling Success* (Authors of Unity) and *What Flavor Is Your Personality?* (Sourcebooks).

Scents stimulate important mental and physical functions. They trigger the release of *neurotransmitters*, chemicals that send signals to the brain. **WHAT SCENTS CAN DO FOR YOU...**

CONTROL APPETITE...

In a study of 105 people, we found that those who inhaled a chocolate-like aroma whenever they felt like eating lost nearly three pounds in two weeks. Another study of 3,193 volunteers found that sniffing banana, green apple or peppermint scents resulted in an average weight loss of 30 pounds in six months.

Sniff these scents often, and smell every food before you eat it. Your brain will perceive that you're eating more, thus suppressing your appetite.

BOOST ROMANCE...

Both men and women are sexually stimulated by scents, but the odors that arouse them aren't the same.

FOR MEN: The smell of lavender or pumpkin pie increases blood flow to the penis by about 40%. The smells of doughnuts, black licorice, vanilla and women's perfume (any scent) are also sexually stimulating to men.

FOR WOMEN: The odors of cucumber and licorice are stimulating. Women are turned off by the smell of cherries, barbecued meat and men's cologne.

REDUCE ANXIETY...

Fresh, natural scents, in general, induce calm. In a study we conducted, volunteers became extremely anxious when they were put in coffin-like tubes—but then calmed down when the tubes were infused with the smells of green apple and cucumber. These odors act on the *limbic* system, the emotional center of the brain.

If you anticipate being in a situation in which you will feel anxious, wash your hair that morning with a green-apple–scented shampoo and/or put a dab of the shampoo in a cloth to take with you.

IMPROVE MEMORY...

People who sniff floral scents increase their retention of new material by 17%.

Sniff a floral odor when learning new material, then smell it again when you want to recall it. This is known as *state-dependent learning.* The material you learn in one state—for example, while smelling roses—will be more accessible when you replicate that state in the future.

■

LUXURIES FOR LESS

Source: **Sue Goldstein,** creator of The Underground Shopper, a multimedia outlet that includes a Dallas-area call-in radio show on shopping and an Internet shopping site at *www.undergroundshopper.com.*

High-quality goods are available now at discounts on the Internet. **MY FAVORITE SITES FOR LUXURY ITEMS...**

• ***Designer clothing and accessories.*** Save at least 50% on new and gently used designer items, including handbags, sunglasses, jeans, pants, tops, dresses, footwear and belts. Brands include Christian Dior, Fendi, Prada and Yves Saint Laurent.

RECENT EXAMPLE: A Prada black nylon and leather shoulder bag was priced at $229.99. The same bag retails for approximately $475. Rodeo Drive Resale, 888-697-3725, *www.rodeodrive resale.com.*

• ***Gourmet coffees and teas.*** Cavallini offers the same exotic blends used at five-star restaurants and resorts. 214-353-0328, *www.cavallinicoffee.com.*

• ***Linens.*** Bedsheet.com sells high-thread-count sheets for up to 70% off retail prices.

RECENT EXAMPLE: A 100% cotton sheet set with a 500-thread count, which typically retails for $299.99, went for $49.99. 800-965-5558, *www.bedsheet.com.*

• ***Skin-care products.*** This company sells skin-care and cosmetic products that usually are available only at spas and doctors' offices. Popular lines include Babor, Frederic Fekkai, Blinc and Cellex-C. 800-709-1865, *www.spalook.com.*

• ***Jewelry.*** Order reproductions of jewelry worn by Hollywood starlets in legendary films.

RECENT SPECIAL: Vivien Leigh's Southern emerald earrings—synthetic green emeralds, each stone 1.03 carats, set in gold-plated sterling silver and surrounded by 10 cubic zirconia stones—for $60. 800-788-5600, *www.thehollywoodcollection.com.*

• ***China, crystal and flatware.*** Great prices on sterling silverware, stainless flatware and silver home accessories, including such top brands as Lenox and Gorham. 800-426-3057, *www.silversuperstore.com.*

■

THE BEST SLOT MACHINES

Source: **Lee Pantano,** gambling expert in Atlantic Highlands, NJ.

Vegas rules are most chaotic for slot machines. In Atlantic City, all machines must return at least 83% of the amount wagered...and a few will return even more than 83%. But in Nevada, one machine might pay back 99%, while the one right next to it pays back only 60%. The bettor's problem is that it's impossible to identify the hot machines. Their placement is the casino's closely guarded secret.

The best-paying machines are usually found third or fourth from the end of a busy aisle, where the most people will see and hear the payoffs.

WORST PAYOFFS: Any machine near the door of a casino.

Among Atlantic City's casinos, the variations are narrower than in Vegas, but they can still be worked for or against you.

■

BETTER SEX

Source: **Domeena Renshaw, MD,** professor, psychiatry and behavioral neurosciences, Loyola University, Maywood, IL.

Exercise your love muscle and you can have better sex. The Kegel exercise, which strengthens the *pubococcygeal* muscle—the muscle responsible for controlling urination—can enhance your love life.

REASON: It can prevent premature ejaculation in men and allow them to make love longer...and help women experience better orgasms.

HOW TO PERFORM THE EXERCISE: For 10 minutes every morning and evening, contract this muscle as if you were holding back the flow of urine. Do 36 contractions at a time and rest for a couple of minutes before beginning again. For best results, practice this exercise for several weeks.

■

GET VIP TREATMENT ON A CRUISE SHIP

Let it be known that you rate A-1 treatment. Your travel agent can do this by writing to the shipping line. Also, the more expensive your cabin, the better service you will generally get.

WHAT YOU CAN EXPECT WHEN YOU ARE TAGGED FOR VIP TREATMENT: Dinner at the captain's table, an invitation to the captain's special cocktail party or perhaps flowers and assorted gifts in your cabin.

• ***Make sure to get a good seat in the dining room.*** Usually, that means in the center, close to the captain's table.

Ask your travel agent to reserve a well-placed table for you in advance. If that can't be done, make sure that as soon as you go aboard ship, you tell the maître d' what you want—and give him a tip.

• ***Have an early talk with your dining-room captain and waiter.*** Ask them what the chef's specialties are. Order those far in advance for your dinners later on in the cruise.

The trick is to know what the kitchen is good at and to give the chef time to prepare it.

• ***Tip the dining-room captain*** and let him know that there's more for him if the service is excellent.

• ***Also give the dining-room waiter, in advance, half the amount you would normally tip him at the end of the cruise*** and indicate that he'll get at least that much more for top-notch service.

He's the man who can get you all sorts of snacks, like fruit, cheeses, sandwiches, iced tea and ice cream—almost any time of day or night. Ask him what is available, and if there is a best time to order these items for your cabin. If you want ice cream at 11 pm every night, tell him in advance, so he can plan accordingly.

Similarly, give your room steward half the tip in advance and let him know that good service will bring a reward.

• ***Book the second sitting for meals.*** That leaves you more time to get ready for dinner after a long day of touring, more time to enjoy your cocktails and less time to kill until the evening activities begin.

■

HOW TO ENJOY RESTAURANTS EVEN MORE

Source: **Bryan Miller,** former food and wine critic for *The New York Times*. He is author of several books on New York City eateries and of *Cooking for Dummies*. IDG Books.

Having a great time at a restaurant depends on many factors—the table, the service, the food, the ambiance, etc. With just a little advance planning, you can greatly improve the odds of enjoying your dining experience.

In the 13 years that I spent as a restaurant critic—mostly at *The New York Times*—and dining out more than 450 times a year, I picked up some inside moves that you can use...

- ***Becoming a regular.*** Restaurants are not democratic institutions. You can become an insider at the restaurants you like by going to them with some regularity, tipping well and chatting with the owner or maître d' so he/she gets to know you.

- ***Finding somewhere new.*** There are 15,000 restaurants in New York City alone. Even the average *avid* diner's universe is rarely more than a dozen. So how can you find somewhere new?

Just walk in—even if you have no plans to eat there. It is amazing how much you can deduce about a restaurant just by spending a minute inside. Is the room lively? Romantic? Suitable for discreet business conversations? Are the patrons enjoying themselves? Is the menu appealing and original? Does the dining room smell good?

- ***Getting a table at trendy restaurants.*** That ultra-hot, hard-to-get-into place-of-the-moment may not be at all hard to get into. Booked to the gills though they may be, great establishments sometimes find themselves with empty tables on weekdays—and even on weekends—from "no-shows."

If you are willing to take a chance, you can walk in without a reservation at 8 pm or later. A restaurant generally holds a table for about 25 minutes, so by that time you may get the table from no-shows who had reserved for 7 pm or 7:30 pm.

NOTE: When you have reservations and are going to be more than 15 minutes late, a phone call to the restaurant is greatly appreciated. Chances are you will be remembered as a considerate customer and the restaurant will respond in kind.

• ***Practical tipping.*** This is the most confusing aspect of eating out. Unless you wind up wearing half your meal or are ignored by the waiter, a standard 15% tip on the total pretax bill is expected. If service is exceptionally good, a tip of 20%—or more—is appropriate.

Payment for captains, who usually supervise teams of waiters, varies. In older and traditional establishments, captains often receive substantial salaries and keep all of their tips. In most new restaurants, the tips are pooled...captains earn only slightly more than waiters—and also depend on tips for much of their income.

The rule of thumb for restaurants with captains is 15% to 18% of the pretax total for waiters plus 5% for captains.

If, however, you want to single out a particular captain or waiter for extraordinary work, you can hand him/her cash upon leaving and say something like, *Thank you...this is for you.* The amount, usually $10 to $20, should be commensurate with the bill.

Maître d's do not usually receive tips unless they have performed specific favors, such as finding you a table on a busy night. In that case, a cash gratuity is warranted, usually from $10 to $20.

Finally, here is a tactic that is rarely employed but can be astoundingly effective in making points with your favorite dining spot. One evening about 12 years ago, I was working as a chef's assistant in a French restaurant when the owner came back and placed a bottle of champagne before us. *The Smiths* (I don't recall their real name) *want to thank you for a great meal,* he said.

You can imagine how well we took care of the Smiths on their subsequent visits.

• ***Strategic complaining.*** Restaurant owners have an adage—*A happy customer tells 10 friends...an unhappy one tells 20.*

The last thing restaurateurs need is an ugly brouhaha in the dining room. They are more inclined to settle any reasonable complaint on the spot—that is, if they are approached with civility, not animosity.

Bring your complaint to an authority, either the manager or the owner. Waiters often have no authority to act above a certain level, so don't waste your time fighting with them.

A well-run establishment will try to make amends for long delays in seating (say, more than 20 minutes) by buying you drinks or perhaps offering a complimentary course or a bottle of wine.

If you do not get satisfaction on the spot, the best recourse is to write a calm, reasonable letter to the owner. Countless times I have seen owners respond with a phone call or a letter and an invitation to return for dinner on the house. This is good customer relations and good business.

• ***Having it your way.*** If you have a special request for a restaurant—say, a vegetarian meal—you should ask when you make the reservation, not when you show up. Doing that at the last minute on a busy night can test the patience of the most genial chef. Occasionally, you may crave a simple dish—perhaps a hamburger...or pasta with only olive oil and garlic—which is not on the menu. In that case, it isn't out of line to ask on the spot if it can be done.

• ***Getting a good table.*** If you are ushered to a table you don't like—actually, there should not be any undesirable tables in good restaurants—politely ask the maître d' if anything else is available.

Restaurants are more flexible in seating than they admit. You may have to wait a bit, but if it enhances your experience, it is worth it.

• ***Beyond Beaujolais.*** Those who are uncomfortable choosing a wine should ask the waiter for his/her suggestion. Be careful to always specify the price range. The standard markup for wine is twice what you would pay in a wine shop...about three times wholesale.

What if you do not like the bottle or glass of wine you chose? If it is off, the restaurant must take it back. If the wine is perfectly fine but not to your liking, tell the waiter. If a restaurant has any class at all, it will replace the wine without comment.

The same applies to food. If you are unhappy with a dish—even if it is well-prepared—you should speak to the waiter or manager. As in the wine example, a professional restaurateur would never risk alienating a customer for the price of one dish.

• ***Good eating on a budget.*** Many restaurants today are offering remarkable bargains during the week with *prix fixe* lunches and dinners. Always ask if there is a special deal like that.

Even better bargains can be had by those who are willing to dine at off hours, say, before 8 pm or after 10 pm. The special menus come and go, so it is always worthwhile for patrons to ask if any exist.

■

16 WAYS TO BE A BETTER GRANDPARENT

Source: **Susan V. Bosak,** Toronto-based author of *How to Build the Grandma Connection.* The Communication Project. She is founding chair of the "Legacy Project." Check out *www.tcpnow.com* for free activities that will help you grow closer to your grandchildren.

Don't take grandparenting for granted. It requires practice and patience. **HERE ARE SOME HELPFUL IDEAS...**

• ***Have a plan.*** Consciously plan the role you want to play in your grandchildren's lives. Discuss your thoughts about being a grandparent with your children, and learn their views. Discuss expectations openly, and you will pave the way for smoother relationships.

When problems do arise, talk about them. Work with your children to find a creative solution.

• ***Keep in touch.*** Whether you're down the block or across the country, maintain regular contact with your grandchildren. It's the foundation of your relationship.

There's no substitute for time spent together. If you live nearby, plan a weekly dinner or outing. If you live far away, visit at least once a year.

Being alone with your grandchildren helps you get to know them better. It can be an afternoon's outing to the park, a parent's night out while you babysit or a few days' stay in your home.

• ***Spend time in the kitchen.*** The kitchen is the place where we're most relaxed, and it is a great place to build relationships with grandchildren.

Prepare a meal together. The conversations that follow will make for some precious memories.

• ***Make them feel welcome.*** Personal touches like a cup with their name or a drawer filled with crayons and toys tell your grandchildren how important they are to you, and how welcome they are in your home.

• ***Use the phone, mail and e-mail.*** Most children love speaking on the phone and receiving letters. A weekly phone call from a long-distance grandparent will give them something to look forward to. For an older child, an unexpected call can be a reassuring reminder that you are there for him/her.

A simple postcard will thrill the young, while a thoughtful letter will be cherished by an older grandchild.

• ***Read aloud to them.*** Grandparents can make an important contribution to their grandchildren's development by taking the time to read aloud to them, particularly when they are very young. Cuddle up in a comfortable chair, and explore the world of the imagination.

• ***Give lots of hugs.*** No matter how old we are, we can all use a hug. A hug is a welcome reminder of how much your grandchild means to you, at any age.

• ***Remember who's in charge.*** Accept your children's decisions as parents with a smile and grace, whether you agree or not. Learning to parent is about learning from mistakes. Be there for your children if they need your insights but only when asked.

You're entitled to opinions about how your grandchildren are raised, but don't meddle and manipulate the relationship. When you have suggestions or disagreements, voice them in a nonjudgmental, supportive way.

• ***When in doubt, listen.*** Listening is *the* most important way grandparents and parents can build a better relationship.

As a grandparent, take the lead in demonstrating how effective listening skills help deal with disagreements and differences. When a problem arises, listen to what everyone has to say.

• ***Think before you speak.*** Don't rush in with advice, comments or solutions—even when they seem obvious. Look beyond words and emotions for the root of problems. Then draw on your experience—and the strength of the family—to offer practical advice from your unique perspective.

• ***Share your family history.*** Telling your grandchildren about your family and its history gives them a sense of who they are. When you share family stories, you're ensuring they'll be handed down.

Whenever possible, share photographs that back up your stories. It's nice to hear about a great-great-grandmother, but even nicer to see a picture of you standing with her, at your grandchild's age.

Give photos of yourself to your grandchildren, especially if you are a long-distance grandparent. Take plenty of pictures when together, and make copies of cherished family photos for older grandchildren to strengthen the family connection.

• ***Tell them about your life.*** As your grandchildren grow, weave memories of your life and experiences into your relationship. A six-year-old just learning to ride would welcome hearing about your first bike. A teenager will enjoy stories of your first love.

• ***Start a shared collection.*** Start your grandchild with a gift to begin a collection, and add to it over time. It can be anything—coins, baseball cards or souvenirs from places you visit. What's important is that it is something special you share and build together.

• ***Give a keepsake.*** Establish a connection between your grandchildren and your past by letting them know that one day a piece of furniture or an heirloom will be theirs. Tell them or write down the reason it is important to you, and its history.

• ***Draw support from your friends.*** When your grandchildren visit for a few days, arrange a get-together with your friends and their grandchildren. This gives you a bit of a break, introduces your grandchildren to your social circle and helps forge a stronger bond between you and your grandchildren.

• ***Learn from your grandparents.*** What do you remember about your grandmother or grandfather? How did they make you feel like such a special person? There is much they can teach you now about what it means, and takes, to be a better grandparent. ■

CHOOSING THE SAFEST SEATS

Source: **Geraldine Frankowski,** former director, Aviation Consumer Action Project, an advocacy group for airline safety and passenger rights, 529 14th St. NW, Washington, DC 20045.

It is a common myth that the safest seats on all commercial aircraft are those next to emergency exits.

REALITY: Aisle seats close to the overwing emergency exits are safer. These seats are commonly in the mid-front section of the plane. If you sit in the window seat next to an emergency exit, you may be worse off in the event of a crash that jams the exit. Aisle seats near several exits give you more escape options in the event of a crash.

LIFESAVING PRECAUTION: When you take your seat in the plane, count and memorize the number of rows to the nearest exits.

REASON: If smoke fills the cabin after a crash, you may have to feel your way in the dark to an exit. This precaution is based on the tactics that crash survivors have actually used to get out of a plane.

■

TRAVEL SMARTS FROM CHARLES LEOCHA

Source: **Charles Leocha,** a Boston-based travel writer. He is author of *Travel Rights*. World Leisure Corp.

Travel rights galore. In more than two decades as a travel writer, I have learned that travelers can get a lot more satisfaction from airlines, rental-car firms and other companies than they ever expected. You just have to know what your rights are. **YOU ARE ENTITLED TO...**

• ***On-the-spot compensation*** if you're involuntarily bumped from a flight in the US or Europe. **YOU GET...**

• One-way fare to your destination if you arrive more than one hour late—two hours on international flights. The maximum is $200.

• 200% of the one-way fare, with a $400 maximum, if you are more than two hours late domestically—or are more than four hours late internationally.

In both cases, you can keep your original ticket and use it on another flight—or get a refund.

IMPORTANT: This is the minimum amount the airline must pay you. You have 30 days to negotiate more.

EXAMPLE: Because being delayed meant I missed a connection and arrived late, the airline also gave me 1,500 frequent-flier miles.

• ***Compensation even if your flight is merely delayed for an hour.*** An airline will usually give you a voucher for lunch or dinner, worth about $10...or a seat on another airline...or put you on a flight to a nearby city.

HELPFUL: If your flight is canceled, or if you just miss it, and you can't get another flight until the next day, ask customer service to book you a "distressed passenger" rate at a local hotel. I did this in Denver during a snowstorm, and a room that cost $100 per night dropped to $39.

• ***Return-date flexibility.*** The outbound segment of a round-trip ticket is generally chiseled in stone. But airlines may allow you to change your return date without a penalty if travel space is available...and the Saturday-night-stay requirement is met.

• ***Vouchers for basics***—clothing, toiletries and sports-equipment rental—if the airline loses your luggage.

EXAMPLE: I once had to attend a formal dinner and my luggage didn't arrive. The airline paid for a tuxedo rental.

If your luggage is lost, the airline is liable for provable consequential damages of up to $3,000 on domestic flights and $9.07 per pound on international flights.

You can submit claims to your homeowner's insurance company if your loss is more than $1,250 or if you are having a problem getting reimbursed, and let them go after your air carrier for reimbursement.

• ***Avoid paying collision damage*** and loss damage insurance for rental cars by paying with the right credit card.

BEST: Diner's Club, 800-234-6377, which provides full-value, primary insurance coverage worldwide for up to 31 days.

If you plan to rent an SUV, minivan or luxury car, make sure the credit card you use covers these "exotic" cars.

• ***Refund on taxes you pay on purchases abroad...***

CANADA: Get back your 7% Goods and Services Tax (GST) by mailing in a refund form from the store within 60 days after purchase. If your claim is for less than $500 (Canadian), make your claim at the border.

You must provide originals of all receipts. You can get a refund on the cost of hotel rooms, but not on gasoline, tobacco, alcohol, meals or car rentals.

EUROPE: To get your Value-Added Tax (VAT) refund, look for stores that display a Tax-Free Shopping sign, and ask for "tax-free shopping cheques." Present these cheques to customs when leaving the country or the European Union.

Then, take your stamped cheques to a cash refund office, located at most airports and at many border crossings in Europe. Funds are converted into US dollars or credited to your credit card. You can also mail cheques to the nearest refund service office after you get home. It is not unusual to be charged an administration fee by the company that is making the refund.

■

10 SECRETS THAT HOTELS DON'T WANT YOU TO KNOW

Source: **Peter Greenberg,** travel editor for NBC's *Today* show, CNBC and MSNBC. He is author of *Hotel Secrets from the Travel Detective.* Villard. *www.petergreenberg.com.*

You want a hotel to be your home away from home, but many aspects of hotel pricing and policy are anything but homey. **HERE'S WHAT YOU NEED TO KNOW...**

GETTING A ROOM...

• ***You get the best rate by calling the hotel's local number,*** not the 800 number, which usually links callers to an off-site centralized call center. Instead of asking for the reservations desk, ask to speak with the manager on duty, the general manager or the director of sales. These people have the authority to negotiate room rates.

It's often possible to beat a hotel's best advertised price by 20%, particularly if you call just a few days before your visit. First, shop around for the best deal on a third-party Internet travel site, such as Expedia.com or Hotels.com. Don't take the deal—just jot it down.

Then call the hotel and explain to a manager or director that you know these Web sites mark up room prices by 20% to 40%. Tell the manager you would like to split the difference—say you'll pay 20% below the price you found on-line. Unless the hotel is filled to capacity, the manager is likely to take you up on your offer.

• ***Everything is negotiable.*** Think parking is overpriced? If the lot looks half empty, offer less than the daily rate. Planning to make a lot of phone calls? Some hotels offer a per-day flat fee for long-distance in the US and local calling—usually $9.95—but you must ask for it.

• ***Rooms are available even when a hotel has no vacancies.*** In any large hotel, a few rooms usually are listed as "out of order" at any given time. The problem might be something as simple as a stain on the carpet or a chair that has been sent out for repairs. If you're desperate for a last-minute room in a hotel that claims to have none available, tell the manager you are willing to take an out-of-order room that has only a minor problem. You might even be able to negotiate a better rate, since the room would otherwise sit empty.

• ***"Guaranteed" rooms aren't really guaranteed.*** When you make a hotel reservation, you are often asked to "guarantee" your room with a credit card—but there's still a chance that the hotel will give away your room if you arrive late. Providing a credit card number improves the odds that your room will be held—but it still pays to call to confirm that you're coming if you won't arrive until after 9 pm.

SAFEGUARDING VALUABLES...

• ***A thief takes one credit card, not your entire wallet.*** It's no secret that crime is common in hotels. The new twist is that some hotel thieves now take just one credit card when they find an unguarded wallet in a room—and leave everything else untouched. Often, the victim doesn't notice the card is missing until the credit line is maxed out.

Travel only with the credit cards that you really need, and check your wallet carefully if you accidentally leave it unattended.

• ***Your bags aren't safe with the bellhop.*** Even in elite hotels, luggage can be stolen right off the luggage carts in the lobby. Although theoretically these bags are in the possession of the bellhop, the hotel assumes no legal responsibility for the loss.

If your bag is going to sit for more than a few minutes, ask that it be placed in a secure room. Keep valuable items in the hotel safe.

HELPFUL: High-end luggage might impress fellow travelers, but it also impresses thieves. The cheaper or uglier your luggage looks, the greater the odds that a thief will target someone else.

• ***It pays to tip the housekeeper every day.*** Exchange a few pleasant words with the housekeeper if you see him/her—and leave a $2 or $3 tip each day. You'll get better service—housekeepers are the most overworked, underpaid, underappreciated people in the hotel, so any gesture will be appreciated.

Knowing the housekeeper also reduces the chances that your room will be burglarized. Dishonest housekeepers are less likely to target guests they have met. If a thief enters your room while it is being cleaned and pretends to be you—a common ruse—the housekeeper will be able to spot the impostor.

MORE INSIDER SECRETS...

• ***Hotel rooms are infested with germs.*** Certain items in hotel rooms never get cleaned. The biggest trouble spots include the TV remote control, telephone and clock/radio. Travel with a package of antibacterial wipes, and clean these items when you arrive.

Also, while reputable hotels provide fresh linens, bedspreads might be cleaned only once every few months. Remove them from the beds as soon as you check in. Ask for clean blankets as soon as you arrive.

• ***Lost-and-found is a great resource for cell-phone users.*** If you use a cell phone, odds are that someday you'll forget to bring your recharging cord or lose it in transit. If you're staying at a hotel, there's no need to buy a replacement. Recharging cords are the number-one item left behind in hotel rooms. Most hotels are willing to lend cords from their lost-and-found—but guests rarely ask.

• ***Not all concierges are really concierges.*** A true concierge is the most connected person in town. He/she can get tickets to sold-out events...reservations to popular restaurants...prescriptions filled in the middle of the night...even a new heel on a shoe by 8 am. (A tip of $10 to $20 usually is appropriate—more if the concierge really worked miracles.) But not all hotels that advertise "concierge service" truly offer it. Many simply assign a regular hotel employee the role each shift.

An elite concierge wears a gold key on his lapel. It's the symbol of Les Clefs d'Or—French for "Keys of Gold"—a prestigious international concierge organization.

■

CONFESSIONS OF A RECOVERING IDIOT

Source: **John Hoover, PhD,** personal coach, organizational behavior consultant and former marriage counselor based in Nashville. He is author of several books, including *How to Live with an Idiot: Clueless Creatures and the People Who Love Them*. Career Press.

Would you like to live more contentedly with the significant idiot in your life—spouse, partner, child, relative, roommate or best friend? You can. But you'll have to get in touch with your own inner idiot first.

I chose a strong word to make a point. Idiots aren't stupid or deliberately mean. They are simply clueless about the powerful effects their words and behavior have on others. This cluelessness can lead to misfired communication, deepening resentment and a deteriorating relationship.

I am a recovering idiot myself. My weakness was thinking that I could solve other people's problems by throwing around advice. But instead of helping, I was driving people—including my wife—away.

IDIOCY REDUCTION...

Helping someone alter idiotic behavior is rarely easy, but it's not impossible. **SUGGESTIONS...**

• ***Avoid empty expectations.*** People often expect their significant idiots to change simply because they want them to. Yet without strong motivation, people do not change.

EXAMPLE: Edith wished Harry would cook more, be nicer to her aunt and watch less TV. For decades, she believed that Harry would read her mind and behave in ways that were contrary to his nature. Finally she gave up and closed herself off emotionally.

Although Edith had mentioned these things, Harry remained blissfully unaware of their importance to her.

KEEPING IT REAL: In a study of couples who had stayed together happily for up to 50 years, one consistent trait was the absence of unrealistic expectations about each other.

• ***Remember the good parts.*** If your significant idiot is your spouse or partner, start with the assumption that you got together for a reason. Excavate layers of calloused resentment until you have unearthed the attraction, affection and respect underneath.

• ***Pay attention.*** Be alert for your significant idiot's readiness to hear your request. Train yourself to become an observant, skilled listener.

• ***Let it go.*** The next time your significant idiot says or does something—again—that makes you crazy, think of the song *Let It Snow* and sing to yourself, "Let it go, let it go, let it go."

Some people will go to their graves trying to prove that they're right. Accept that you can both be right in your own way. Creating a more tolerant, forgiving atmosphere relaxes tension immeasurably.

• ***Take inventory.*** You're part of this relationship, too. Identify aspects of your personality that are tough to live with. Enlist a friend's help. Naming your faults may be easier for someone else.

THEN DECIDE: Do you care enough about your significant idiot to change?

THE SEVEN RELATIONAL SINS...

To defuse idiotic behavior, avoid committing the seven relational sins...

• ***Anger.*** It's a natural emotion and can be dealt with.

MISTAKES: To deny that you are angry...to choose anger over healthier alternatives.

You already know what makes you angry, so use anticipation as an antidote. Give yourself the option to say, "I was aware that this might happen. It's not the end of the world." Or, "I knew this was possible. On to Plan B."

• ***Blaming.*** Blaming usually takes place in the heat of the argument and only makes things worse.

SOLUTION: Disengage from battle. Announce that you're taking a time-out because the conversation is not working, but you'll be back after sorting out your thoughts.

Disappear, write down some solutions and come back. Keep the conversation going. Time can heal many things if you let it.

• ***Criticizing.*** Most people have been conditioned to respond to negativity with more negativity. Criticism breeds criticism.

If you're about to say something negative when feeling disappointed in your significant idiot, think of something positive and pay a compliment instead. Bingo!—you've de-escalated the hostility in the air.

BONUS: A person who is being complimented can't deflect criticism back onto you.

• ***Denial.*** Failing to acknowledge the truth is like holding beach balls under water. They keep popping back up.

The energy required to hold the truth beneath the surface is better spent on accepting what it represents—the reality of who you and your closest relations really are—and working from there.

• ***Judging.*** Looking down on your significant idiot only widens the gap between you.

DISARMING: Forgiving the offender. To forgive is to let something go and let it float away...to start things moving again.

• ***Resentment.*** Idiotic behavior breeds resentment, which is entirely unproductive. You may have heard the saying that harboring resentment is like drinking a cup of poison and waiting for the other person to die.

Unless friction in a long relationship is discussed openly and honestly, the resulting hostility won't go away. But when people work at it, the results can be phenomenal.

MY RECOMMENDATION: Be lovingly relentless in expressing your (reasonable) wishes.

EXAMPLE: Sue says, "You never take me dancing." Stan replies, "It thrills me to take you dancing. I thought it embarrassed you to be with such a bad dancer." Sue says, "I thought you were embarrassed. I love dancing with you. Let's go!" Misunderstandings kept them captive for too long.

The risk of expressing what you want is that the person won't change. But if you don't try, you're inviting defeat.

• ***Shaming.*** A step beyond criticizing behavior, shame is an assault on a person's character—a guilt trip, hardly a loving (or effective) way to change behavior.

EXAMPLE: With a sigh, Dinah tells Oscar, "Shirley's husband takes out the garbage without being asked."

Instead of belittling Oscar by implication, Dinah might praise him for doing other household tasks independently...and state how pleased she would be if that applied to the garbage, too.

BE PATIENT...

Whatever is causing cluelessness in your significant idiot—and yourself—didn't happen overnight. The attitudinal adaptations required to live a happier, more fulfilling life will take time, too. Identify and pursue them—together.

■

HOW TO PAY LESS FOR EVERYTHING!

4 

HOW TO PAY LESS FOR EVERYTHING!

HOW TO SAVE $3,000 A YEAR ON GROCERIES

Source: **Phil Lempert,** editor of Supermarketguru.com, a Web site that focuses on food and health news; host of the syndicated radio program *Shopping Smart* and food editor for NBC's *Today* show. He is also author of *Phil Lempert's Supermarket Shopping and Value Guide.* Contemporary Books.

The key to cutting your grocery bills in a super-competitive marketplace is to think *value*...not just *price.* Here are some surefire ways to get the most from your shopping excursions—in every aisle, every time you shop.

GET TO KNOW YOUR SUPERMARKET...

Value is a balance of four factors—quality, price, selection and service. Supermarket customers visit, on average, two different supermarkets a week and several different stores each month in search of the best value. But—53% of shoppers say they dislike supermarket shopping...and 14% downright *hate* it.

MY AIM: To help you get the best value from your supermarket *and* help you have more fun grocery shopping.

• ***Choose one store to be your regular supermarket.*** With more than 35,000 products available on most supermarket shelves, there's no reason to keep switching stores.

• ***Front-end electronic marketing programs*** are similar to frequent-shopper programs, but members are rewarded based on the amount they spend. Such programs are often one part of a broader preferred-shopper program, rather than a standalone benefit.

• ***Purchase-triggered coupon programs,*** also called purchase-activated coupon programs, issue coupons at the checkout register that are good for future purchases at that particular chain of stores. The coupons are "triggered" by the purchases you have just made. These programs do not keep track of your personal shopping habits.

EXAMPLE: If you just bought Brand X peanut butter, you may receive a coupon for Brand Y peanut butter or a larger size of Brand X...or a jar of jelly.

• ***Instant electronic discounts*** are also called "paperless coupons." Customers who use their membership cards at the checkout register automatically receive discounts on products that have been identified in mailers or by signs on the shelves. Some supermarkets also offer customers discounts at neighboring businesses, entries in contests and other electronic rewards.

• ***Meet the store manager and/or customer service manager.*** Be sure to tell him/her that you are a long-time regular customer. Mention what you like about the store—and suggest improvements. **ASK THE FOLLOWING QUESTIONS...**

- What are the best/worst times to shop here?
- What are your biggest sale items?
- What day do your weekly sales begin?
- Can I get an advance copy of your newspaper and circular ads and a schedule of in-store sales, product samplings and promotional events?
- How do I join your frequent-shopper program, and if there is a fee, will you waive it? (Usually, the answer is *yes.*)

• ***Get to know the staff in the store—and save $100.*** Exchanging friendly greetings with the people who work where you shop will always make your supermarket visits more enjoyable

—and can save you $100 a year or more. Introduce yourself to the cashiers and to the people in the produce section, deli, bakery and other departments—*and tell them you are interested in sales and special offers.*

Once they get to know you, the supermarket staff will point out new products, special promotions and sales. They will direct you to in-store coupons, newspaper or circular coupons and rebate offers.

UNDERSTAND MARKETING EFFORTS—AND TRICKS...

• ***Use coupons—and save $300.*** If you use just 10 manufacturer's coupons every week, at an average of about 60 cents each, you'll save more than $300 a year.

• ***Buy store brands—and save $2,000.*** Switching to your supermarket's "private label" or "store brand" is one of the best ways to save money with no loss of quality.

In most cases, when you compare the ingredients list of "store-brand" products to those of the national brands, you will find that the quality is equal, if not superior, to the name-brand product. Often, store brands are made by the same manufacturers as national brands. You'll have to try store-brand products to see if you like them.

If you spend $135 to $140 a week on groceries, you can save more than $2,000 a year by switching to store brands.

• ***Outsmart supermarket display techniques.*** **DON'T FALL FOR COMMON SUPERMARKET DISPLAY TRICKS...**

• Placing the highest-priced items at eye level.

• Piling up end-of-aisle displays with products that are close to their expiration date but are not necessarily on sale.

• Grouping products to provoke impulse buying, like chips, dips and soft drinks.

• Making attractive arrangements of delicious precut fruit or salad items that are far more expensive than the unsliced versions.

• Creating an "international" cheese table or deli display when the same prepackaged products are available in the dairy case for much less.

• Placing staple items, such as milk, in the back of the store, forcing you to walk past the rest of the merchandise.

STRATEGY: If you need just a gallon of milk, avoid temptation by walking down an aisle stocked with items you rarely buy, such as automobile supplies, pet food or school supplies.

• ***Stick to your list—and save $300.*** Finally, the supermarket shopper's must—always shop with a list and control your impulse buys. This is an easy way to save $300 a year.

I limit myself to three impulse purchases per shopping trip, but otherwise stick carefully to my list. This strategy guarantees that I always have fun while I'm shopping—but I never exceed my budget.

■

HOW TO SAVE HUNDREDS OF DOLLARS

Source: Consumer electronics expert **Robert Silva,** based in La Mesa, CA. Since 1999, he has written for About.com and currently serves as its home-theater guide. *hometheater.about.com.*

Every year, billions of dollars worth of brand-name appliances and electronics are returned to retailers and manufacturers. Consumers return items because of shipping damage and minor defects or simply because they changed their minds. In the past, since these products could no longer be marketed legally as "new," they were destroyed or sent to liquidators. But retailing has become so competitive that manufacturers now "refurbish" returned goods—repairing and repackaging them—and then sell them as high-quality, used merchandise.

SAVINGS: Up to 80% off retail price.

"Refurbs"—from cameras and laptop computers to DVD players and golf clubs—come with a limited choice of features and colors and may not have the latest technology, but their prices make them attractive bargains.

How to shop for refurbs...

• ***Find out how the manufacturer or retailer defines "refurbished."*** There are no federal regulations for labeling these goods, which also may be called "factory reconditioned," "open-box" or "preowned," but many sellers will tell you if you ask.

THE BEST REFURBS ARE...

• Items that have been returned unused. Most major retailers have a 30-day return policy for their products.

• Otherwise-sound goods that had cosmetic damage, perhaps scratches or dents. The internal components usually are put into a new cabinet or casing.

• Overstock items. These are typically older models that need to be cleared off store shelves.

Less desirable refurbs...

• Demonstration units. These floor models are used in stores, at trade shows or for product reviews. They often have suffered substantial wear and tear.

• Defective products. These items already have been repaired, which may or may not have fixed the problem.

• ***Look for a strong parts-and-labor warranty and return policy.*** The product should come with a 45-day warranty and a 14-day return policy.

• ***Make sure the refurb comes with all the basic components of a new product.*** Check the model and configuration of the newest version of the item on the manufacturer's Web site or in the owner's manual to make sure that your model comes with everything you need. For example, some refurbished electronics may be sold without the necessary cables, headphones, software, etc.

■

HOW TO TRAVEL FREE

Source: **Robert William Kirk,** author of *You Can Travel Free.* Pelican Publishing Co.

Instead of traveling cheap, you could be traveling free—from transportation by air—or sea—to lodgings, meals and entertainment. Most free travel requires no special skills, credentials or contacts. And it can be just as luxurious—and often more pleasurable—than the most expensive paid vacation.

Cruise lines generally offer a free passage to anyone who recruits 10 to 15 paying passengers. (Many airlines offer similar deals.) If you can't lure that many customers, you can get a prorated reduction on your fare.

You can also cruise free as an expert in a pertinent subject. Historians, anthropologists, naturalists and ornithologists are in especially high demand. Your job on the cruise would be to present a series of lectures and to be available for informal questioning. It helps to have a PhD (or at least a Master's) and to have published articles on the subject, but an affable personality and a willingness to share your knowledge with others can stretch your credentials. After your first cruise in this capacity, a good reference will ease the way at other lines.

Free cruises are available to doctors and nurses willing to be on 24-hour call (a salary is an added inducement)...to athletic directors and coaches who can help organize recreational activities...to musicians and entertainers who will perform...to cosmetologists who can barter their services.

There is also a strong demand for "hosts"—distinguished single gentlemen who are usually 55 years and older. They serve by dining and dancing with the many unattached older women taking these vacation cruises. In addition to free room and board, hosts may make use of an unlimited bar tab available for themselves and their new female friends.

■

SAVE MONEY ON ALMOST EVERYTHING

Source: **Linda Bowman,** author of the *More for Your Money* series of guides, including *Free Food & More* (Probus Professional) and *Free Stuff & Good Deals for Folks Over 50* (Santa Monica Press).

A few dollars saved here and there can add up very quickly. **HERE ARE SOME RESOURCES THAT WILL HELP YOU CUT COSTS WITHOUT SACRIFICING...**

UTILITIES/ENERGY...

• ***For a free evaluation of your energy usage,*** call your local utilities company. Many utilities also *give away* energy-saving devices, such as low-flow shower heads, water heater blankets and fluorescent bulbs.

• ***Repair major appliances yourself.***

HOW: Contact manufacturers' customer service for repair instructions.

- Whirlpool, 800-253-1301, *www.whirlpool.com*
- Electrolux, 800-896-9756, *www.electrolux.com*

• ***Gather free firewood from any of our 155 national forests.*** Contact your regional office of the USDA Forest Service for a permit, which allows you up to six units of downed or dead wood. At the going rate of about $120 a cord, this will save you money.

• ***Install a water restrictor for your shower.*** It saves thousands of gallons of water a year. Check with your utility for a free restrictor.

HOME AND HEALTH-CARE PRODUCTS...

• ***Take advantage of refund/rebate offers.*** Take the time to save UPC symbols, labels and receipts. The savings can easily reach hundreds of dollars a year.

GOOD SOURCE OF OFFERS: Supermarket and drugstore bulletin boards.

• ***Ask for free samples at department store cosmetics counters.*** Say you need to try products before you buy, and you'll receive handfuls of high-priced makeup, skin-care products and fragrances.

WATCH FOR: Fine print in magazine ads offering free samples of perfumes or moisturizers if you write or call an 800 number.

• ***Have your hair cut, colored, permed or styled at a cosmetology school.*** Students are closely supervised by expert instructors.

SAVINGS: About 60% less than a salon. The average American woman spends $360 a year at hair salons, so expect to save $216.

• ***Get routine dental care at a dental school.*** Services, including orthodontics, at the country's 57 dental school clinics are high-quality and 60% less expensive than normal dentists' fees.

• ***Ask your doctor for free samples of medications whenever you get a prescription.*** Most doctors have plenty to give away.

HOME ENTERTAINMENT...

• ***Take advantage of free magazine offers.*** Don't throw away subscription invitations from periodicals. Most publications will send you a free issue, and then begin your subscription unless you cancel.

KEY: Write "cancel" on the invoice, and mail it back. The postage is almost always paid, and you owe nothing.

• ***Use your public library*** to borrow books, records, audiotapes, videotapes, DVDs, even artwork.

• ***Order free publications from your favorite manufacturers.*** Quite a few food companies offer free cookbooks, including Sun-Maid Raisins, Smucker's and Ragu...as do a number of trade organizations, including Meat & Livestock Australia (Australian lamb cookbook).

EXAMPLES: Eastman Kodak of Rochester, New York, offers free booklets on photography...and United Van Lines offers brochures related to planning a move.

Check package labels for the location of company headquarters. Then contact the company's customer service department.

■

HOME-REPAIR GRANTS

Source: Rural Development Agency, Washington, DC, or one of their local offices. *www.rurdev.usda.gov.*

Homeowners age 62 and older can qualify for a lifetime maximum of $7,500 to repair their homes.

OTHER REQUIREMENTS: The home must be in a rural area—population under 20,000—and applicants must show that they cannot repay the money.

■

SHREWDER ON-LINE SHOPPING: FIND GREAT ITEMS AT BARGAIN PRICES

Source: **Hillary Mendelsohn,** founder, thepurplebook®, *www.thepurplebook.com,* Beverly Hills, CA. She is author of *thepurplebook: the definitive guide to exceptional on-line shopping,* which lists more than 1,700 on-line shopping sites in 19 different categories. Warner.

Shopping on-line takes you outside of the old, familiar stores and malls and brings a global bazaar right to your door. The variety of goods available on-line is breathtaking—with many items that you'll never see at the mall—and prices are often lower than you would pay elsewhere.

Still, on-line shopping can be filled with perils. You may be shopping with merchants you've never dealt with before (some of them half a world away), you don't get to see items before buying them and identity thieves could steal your most personal information.

Here's how to be a savvy and safe on-line shopper...

FINDING WHAT'S BEST ON-LINE...

While virtually every mass-market retailer sells on-line today, the beauty of the Internet is being able to find off-beat merchants selling hard-to-find treasures. Whatever you're into, from gourmet foods to sports memorabilia, it's available on-line. **HERE'S HOW TO FIND IT...**

• ***Know how to search.*** I love Google, but my favorite search engine for finding goods on-line is Dogpile (*www.dogpile.com*). Once you enter what you're looking for, Dogpile offers invaluable tips to help you refine your search. It also provides fewer results to wade through than most search engines. Once you decide to buy an item, such as a specific brand and style of shoes, go to BizRate.com (*www.bizrate.com*) to see which on-line merchant offers the best price. Take into account shipping prices when doing your comparison.

• ***Look for contact information.*** The hardest thing to find on-line is a telephone number that will let you make personal contact with the merchant—to ask questions, follow up on orders and resolve disputes. I won't list a site in my book that doesn't have a listed phone number.

HINT: If a site doesn't have a listed phone number, sometimes you can find it by searching *http://yp.yahoo.com.*

• ***Demand quick, easy shopping.*** You should be able to complete the on-line transaction without a lot of wasted time and keystrokes. Avoid any site that requires you to enter tons of information (name, address, e-mail address, etc.) just to find out if an item is in stock.

• ***Go with your gut.*** If the site seems flimsy—without all the information you need to make your selection—skip it.

HOW TO HAGGLE...

You'll often pay less for an item on-line, since many sites don't charge sales tax and may offer free shipping. Mass-market retailers are doing more to encourage on-line shopping—including offering discounts. If you register with them, you can get e-mail about special offers, advance notification of sales, plus coupons and discounts.

Even if a store doesn't specifically mention discounts to on-line shoppers, it may be possible to negotiate a better deal for yourself.

Most sites include a comments box on the order form. Use that box to ask for a lower price, or free shipping or gift wrapping.

Don't expect a biggie like Wal-Mart or L.L. Bean to bargain with you on-line. But a smaller retailer may be willing to deal...especially if the item is one of a kind, such as a piece of handmade jewelry.

HOW TO SHOP SAFELY...

Although most identity theft does not take place on the Internet, you still want to exercise caution. **HERE'S HOW...**

- ***Patronize sites that use a secure server.*** This means that any information you enter on-line is encrypted before being transmitted. The standard for security is 128-bit encryption, and sites that offer it will usually display that information prominently.

Favor sites that display the VeriSign Secured Seal to indicate they use a secure server. The seal is in red, with a black checkmark.

- ***Pay with a credit card—rather than with a debit card.*** Your bank card number and often your PIN must be transmitted with a debit card transaction, making you vulnerable to hackers. Also, if there is a problem with the merchandise or the billing, or if the order was never shipped, you can withhold payment for the purchase from the credit card issuer. With a debit card, the money comes out of your bank account the instant you complete the transaction.

HOW TO TOUCH THE MERCHANDISE...

The biggest problem with on-line shopping is that you can't hold the item in your hand and examine it for color, size, quality, etc.

SOLUTION: Use sites that do the best job of illustrating and describing what you're buying.

If color is a factor, for example, you'll want to be shown all the colors in which the item is offered. With clothing, you'll want a chart of sizes, an explanation of how the items are sized and a guide to help you pick the size you'll need.

IMPORTANT: Since there's always a certain amount of guesswork involved in shopping on-line, the merchant's return and exchange policies are critical. You must be able to return the item within a reasonable amount of time—at least 30 days—and get a full refund rather than just a credit against another purchase.

FOREIGN SHOPPING...

You're not limited to the US when shopping on-line. You can buy from merchants anywhere in the world. However, I do set a much higher standard for the international sites that I list in my book.

The site must be in English. It must offer a currency converter, showing the price of the item in both dollars and in the local currency. The site must also offer size-conversion charts so you understand the difference between US sizes and European or British sizes.

IMPORTANT: The cost of shipping must be reasonable, even if the item is coming from far away. If you're not careful, the cost of shipping can exceed the value of the item. The best international sites keep their shipping costs close to what it would cost to have the item shipped from a domestic supplier.

HOW TO RESOLVE COMPLAINTS...

Most of the time, your on-line shopping will go without a hitch. Merchants have been selling on-line long enough to have ironed out many of the issues that caused trouble at the beginning.

Still, things can go wrong. Anticipate trouble by collecting all the documents you might need in case something does.

Save all records of your on-line order, including any e-mail the company sends you to confirm your purchase. Print the order page before you press the submit button. That will give you a copy of the order page just as you prepared it, with the color, size and shipping method that you selected.

If there's a complaint that can't be resolved with the merchant or you think you've been a victim of fraud, complain to the Federal Trade Commission (FTC), which polices on-line shopping.

Visit the FTC Web site at *www.ftc.gov* to see what your rights are and for instructions on filing a complaint. Click on "econsumer.gov," a special corner of the FTC site that handles cross-border on-line shopping complaints.

SOME OF MY FAVORITE SITES...

These sites are both useful and user-friendly...

- ***Accessories.*** Hats in the Belfry (*www.hatsinthebelfry.com*). Every hat you can imagine is here, from dignified headwear to a purple Mad Hatter's top hat.
- ***Entertainment.*** Audible.com (*www.audible.com*) offers a huge selection of audio books available for download.
- ***Epicurean.*** Pop's Wines & Spirits (*www.popswine.com*) has a great selection. Petrossian Paris (*www.petrossian.com*) sells caviar, pâté and other gourmet delicacies.
- ***Gadgets/electronics.*** B&H (*www.bhphotovideo.com*) bills itself as the world's leading retailer of all imaging equipment at discount prices.
- ***Health/beauty.*** Sephora (*www.sephora.com*) puts thousands of high-quality beauty products at your fingertips.
- ***Home/garden.*** Cooking.com (*www.cooking.com*). Everything on this site is so well laid out that even a novice cook will have no trouble navigating it.
- ***Pets.*** Doctors Foster & Smith (*www.drsfostersmith.com*) offers all your pet needs plus the expert advice of veterinarians.
- ***Stationery/gifts.*** Star Treatment (*www.startreatment.com*) has wonderful gift baskets.
- ***Travel.*** Magellan's (*www.magellans.com*) has appliances and accessories for every travel need.

FOREIGN SITES...

Check out these foreign Web sites for some unique finds...

- ***Ancient Art On-line*** (*www.ancientart.co.uk*), based in London, has everything ancient from Roman coins to Ming dynasty pottery.
- ***Brora Scottish Cashmere*** (*www.brora.co.uk*). This London–based site sells cashmere goods for men, women and children.
- ***Charles Tyrwhitt*** (*www.ctshirts.co.uk*) bills itself as "England's largest maker of quality shirts through the Internet and mail order."
- ***Histoires de Parfums.com*** (*www.histoiresdeparfums.com*). This Paris–based perfumery is "dedicated to creating prestige fragrances according to the finest traditional French methods."

■

NOW IS THE TIME TO GET SERIOUS ABOUT CUTTING TELEPHONE BILLS

Source: **Stephen Semprevivo,** president, LowerMyBills.com. This Santa Monica, CA–based company provides Web users with a free comparison of prices in 18 categories, including communications, home mortgages, insurance, credit cards and auto loans. *www.lowermybills.com.*

My company, which helps consumers compare prices of phone and other services, has records showing that most households can lower phone bills by $400 a year—and often much more.

Before making a decision on any type of land line or cellular service, check your bills for the past six to 12 months to see where you spent the most money—on local, intrastate, interstate or overseas calls. Each type of call is usually billed at a different rate.

Only when you know your spending pattern can you shop for companies that provide the specific services that you use most often. **COST-CUTTING STRATEGIES...**

THINK SMALL...

You may have grown up with the huge Ma Bell, but a growing number of small carriers now offer long-distance service at bargain prices. My experience tells me that most customers are as satisfied with these companies as they are with such major carriers as Bell South, MCI, SBC, Sprint and Verizon.

In fact, many of the alternative companies do business simply by buying and reselling long-distance capacity from the country's best-known carriers. Still, if you have doubts about signing up with a little-known company, check with your local Better Business Bureau (*www.bbb.com*) or your state attorney general's office.

Nearly all alternative carriers beat the majors in price, some offering domestic long distance for less than three cents a minute. That's a couple of cents cheaper than the best deals from most major carriers.

Because few alternative companies spend much on advertising, they may be difficult to find. In addition to using my Web site, *www.lowermybills.com*, you can find these carriers by keying in "long-distance plans" in Google or other search engines.

Many are also listed in the Yellow Pages under "Telephone Communication Services" and "Long-Distance Telephone Services."

Alternative carriers with low prices include Pioneer Telephone (888-492-6878, *www.pioneertelephone.com*), PowerNet Global (877-550-5918, *www.pngnet.com*) and Total Call International (*www.totalcallusa.com*, 800-330-6895).

When considering any type of carrier, don't be influenced just by the low rates that appear on its Web site. Instead, make sure that the rates will actually lower your bills when they're applied to your specific calling patterns.

Many phone companies offer calling plans that charge a minimum monthly fee for long-distance service, usually $3.95 to $12.95, while some have no minimum fee.

To find out whether you'll save money on a plan with a minimum charge, again, apply it to your calling patterns.

STAY FLEXIBLE...

Don't sign up for any type of phone service unless the contract clearly cites a trial period during which you can cancel without a penalty. Most carriers are glad to oblige, although their ads don't always make that clear.

Trial periods are essential because problems often do not become apparent until you've used the service for a while.

EXAMPLES: Cell phones that don't work in certain areas or long-distance rates that unexpectedly rise.

ALSO: Don't sign a phone contract of longer than one year, especially for cellular service. Your phone needs could change, or rates could unexpectedly decline, making them lower than the ones you locked into.

LOOK TO THE NET...

Computer users have long been able to make calls over the Internet, but the technology was cumbersome. Today, problems have largely been solved.

Two leading Internet telephone companies are Vonage (866-243-4357, *www.vonage.com*) and Deltathree (*www.iconnecthere.com*).

Vonage, for example, offers unlimited local and domestic long-distance calls for $24.99 a month (plus tax) and a start-up charge of about $45, depending on locality. There is no contract.

Customers also need broadband Internet service, which usually costs $30 to $50 a month.

The monthly charge at Vonage includes voice mail, caller ID, call waiting, call forwarding and three-way calling.

TYPICAL OVERSEAS RATES: Three cents a minute to London or Paris.

The start-up charge includes an adapter that links your computer's broadband Internet connection to phones in your house.

Early technology required Internet phone users to sit at a computer. Today, Vonage, Deltathree and similar companies let customers use their regular phones—even cordless ones.

This makes the service nearly indistinguishable from that of conventional telephones.

DRAWBACKS: The quality of the connection may occasionally not be as clear as it is with traditional land-line phones. (A representative at the Internet phone company can arrange for you to hear the quality of the connection to help you decide if it is suitable for your needs.) Also, if the electricity goes out, you'll lose phone service.

AVOID CELL TRAPS...

Though competition may be waning among providers of land lines, it's still hot in the cell phone business.

Don't fall into the trap of rushing to sign up for bargain cellular service before making sure that you'll actually use what you're buying.

Text messaging, Internet access, three-way calling and caller ID can seem attractive at first, but these features often go unused while adding $15 to $30 to your monthly bill.

Before contracting for cellular service, also ask the company to fully describe the areas where you can use it without incurring high roaming charges. Some companies may say the area includes an entire city or county, but in reality, there can be pockets within that area where connections aren't available without roaming fees. Ask for a map if there's any doubt.

CONSIDER CARDS...

Long-distance calling cards allow you to make inexpensive domestic and foreign calls from any line by keying in a user-ID number.

EXAMPLE: Long-distance calls in the US are as low as 0.9 cents a minute with a Nobel USA card (888-520-9215, *www.nobelcom.com*).

Cards are a big advantage if the type of call you want to make isn't included in the calling plan with your regular carrier. Or if you're outside your cellular phone's roaming area, you can save money by using a calling card from a pay phone.

DISADVANTAGES: Many cards charge a weekly "maintenance" fee or a connection charge for each use. Others charge a fee for use at a pay phone.

Since calling cards are usually no more than $10 or $20, it won't cost you much to try several different ones to see how much they save you.

■

HOW MARY HUNT SAVES BIG MONEY ON BIG PURCHASES AND YOU CAN, TOO

Source: **Mary Hunt,** editor of *Debt-Proof Living, www.debtproofliving.com.* She is author of a dozen books on saving money, including *Everyday Cheapskate's Greatest Tips: 500 Simple Strategies for Smart Living* (Running Press) and *Live Your Life for Half the Price—Without Sacrificing the Life You Love* (DPL).

Big-ticket purchases can strain your budget for years. **HERE'S HOW TO SAVE HUNDREDS TO THOUSANDS OF DOLLARS ON APPLIANCES, ELECTRONICS AND MORE...**

• ***Anticipate big purchases.*** Many people avoid thinking about when they might need to make a big purchase. Then once the time comes, they make a hasty decision. Instead, plan ahead.

Reputable dealers will gladly tell you how long a big-ticket item is likely to last.

EXAMPLES: Dishwasher, 10 years...top-load washer, 10 years ...front-load washer, 14 years...refrigerator, 12 to 15 years... mattress, eight to 10 years...laptop computer, three years (if you use the computer every day).

As soon as you buy a big-ticket item, earmark a portion of your monthly savings for its replacement, based on how long you expect it to last. When an item is approaching the end of its useful life, keep an eye out for sales on new models.

SMART: Add years to the life of big-ticket items with regular maintenance. Service the lawn mower each year—change the oil and sharpen the blade. Run a gallon of vinegar through the washing machine every few months to remove mineral buildup from hard water. Flip mattresses regularly to even out the wear patterns.

• ***Use credit only if you expect the item to last more than three years.*** Also, make sure that you can pay it off in less than three years—you don't want to run the risk of problems before you finish paying for the item.

ITEMS THAT YOU SHOULDN'T BUY WITH CREDIT: Laptop computers, baby cribs, MP-3 players, video game systems. After three years, these items are likely to be worth less than the amount you still owe on them. You never want to get trapped into making monthly payments on an expensive product that you rarely use.

• ***Match quality to need.*** Buy only big-ticket items that you truly need, and avoid paying for features that you will never actually use.

EXAMPLE: A few years ago, I needed a new vacuum cleaner. I saw an ad for a high-end model ($500) that had received a top-quality rating. It turned out to be the vacuum that rated best in picking up animal hairs and dander from deep-pile carpeting. Since I have neither pets nor thick carpets, I opted for another model with good ratings that cost half as much, and it does everything that I need it to do.

• ***Negotiate for discounts.*** Stores need to turn over their inventory regularly. Hand the salesperson your phone number or business card and say, "If you need to meet a sales quota in the next month or two and you can help me get a better discount on this stereo system or tell me when it will be on sale, give me a call." Also ask for free shipping and/or free assembly.

Once you've agreed on a price, request a further discount—for example, 10%—for paying in cash. You're more likely to get this discount from local retailers, who want to avoid the fees they have to pay when you use your credit card, than from national chains, which have bigger sales volume. Although you will miss out on credit card company protections, these are typically very limited and a discount for paying cash is hard to beat.

• ***Look for a "price guarantee" policy*** that promises to match any competitor's price on the same item for at least 30 days following the purchase. Keep an eye out for sales during this period. Most national retail chains have price-match guarantees.

• ***Avoid extended warranties.*** Service contracts are tempting because big-ticket items can be expensive to repair or replace. But these agreements cover the middle years of a product's life—after the initial warranty but before "old age" sets in—when it is unlikely to experience problems. It rarely pays to purchase extended warranties for long-lasting appliances, such as dishwashers, washers and dryers.

Only take the extended warranty on items that are known to have high failure rates in the first few years, such as treadmills and laptop computers. The warranty should last at least as long as you plan to use the item—in some cases, this might require you to renew the warranty. The cost of the warranty should not exceed 20% of the purchase price.

HELPFUL: If you make a purchase with an American Express card, one year is added for free to any manufacturer's warranty that covers less than five years.

• ***Comparison shop on-line.*** **HERE ARE A FEW OF MY FAVORITE RESOURCES...**

• *www.consumerreports.org*, which provides product ratings (a one-year subscription is $26).

• *www.epinions.com*. Customer reviews of products.

• *www.google.com/products*, a product search engine. Type in the specific item, and get a listing of all prices for the item on the Internet, including prices from on-line auctions.

• *www.salescircular.com*. Lets you look for the best price in your state at Best Buy, Circuit City, CompUSA, Kmart, Office Depot, OfficeMax, RadioShack, Sears, Staples, Target and Wal-Mart, as well as local-area retailers.

• *www.gotapex.com*. Super deals on computer equipment.

■